A Heart
Exchange

A Heart Exchange

THE STORY OF
SISTER JOYCE BLUM, FSPA

Tim Sullivan
Patricia Graeve Michels
and Charlotte Willenborg

A Heart Exchange

ISBN: 978-1-4951-2668-0

To order additional copies of this book, please contact:

Patricia Graeve Michels
1325 Elmwood Rd
Panama, IA 51562-6604

e-mail: jpmichelsfarm@gmail.com

Dedication

**To all the new friends we met
as we journeyed together in the creation
of our Heart Exchange.**

Authors' Note

Several years ago the six Catholic parishes in Shelby County Iowa began exploring the idea of having a sister parish in Central America. Our initial contact was with a parish in Honduras, and we put a notice in our church bulletins inviting any interested parishioners to join us for a trip to visit the parish. We got a call from a Sister Joyce Blum who was originally from Shelby County but was now living in Des Moines. She said she would love to travel to Honduras with our group. We didn't really know too much about Joyce, but she spoke Spanish and had lots of experience in Central America so we said, she was welcome to come along. And just that simply, the adventure began.

It does not take long to become friends with Sister Joyce. She is a larger than life woman who loves people. As we began to learn a little about her life, we thought someone should write a book about this lady. We had never known anyone that had so completely allowed the Spirit to lead them through life. I am not sure who in our group suggested that we would have to write the book, but maybe we allowed a little of her openness to the Spirit to influence us.

We went to Central America to explore the people and places where Joyce had worked. We not only learned more about Sister Joyce but also about the history, culture, geography, and people of El Salvador. It is a fascinating and in many ways a tragic story. We discovered the Catholic Church was at the heart of the peoples' struggle leading up to El Salvador's civil war, and Sister Joyce was a leading figure in the work of the church. The only reason she is not well known is because she was not murdered by the government like so many other religious.

When she returned to the United States, her life was no longer in constant danger, but she was no less led by the Spirit. She continued to serve the people on the margins of society in such intimate ways it is difficult for the rest of us to imagine. We suspect people who may know Joyce will be amazed by the new things they will learn about her life.

The book is now complete, but Sister Joyce continues her ministry work and her involvement with the Shelby County Catholic church's efforts in Central America. Any proceeds from this book will go to support those efforts.

We hope that Sister Joyce's story inspires you to open your heart to God's Spirit in some small way as it has for us.

The Authors

Tim Sullivan, Patricia Graeve Michels and Charlotte Willenborg

Acknowledgments

We would like to thank the many people who helped us with this book: Special thanks to our team of editors; Lindsey Greer, Dawn Grabs, Judy Clark, and Fr. Jack McClure, C.PP.S. who all did a great job with a challenging task. We would like to thank Tom Turkle for graciously volunteering to lay out the book for printing, and sharing his knowledge of the publishing process. We are grateful to the Franciscan Sisters of La Crosse for their support, including a generous financial grant to help cover costs. The hospitality and the local knowledge of Father Jose Reynaldo Hernadez in El Salvador were most appreciated. We would like to thank Monsignor Carpio for sharing his home, knowledge, and giving us a day of relaxation on the beach in El Salvador. It was a special pleasure that Monsignor Ricardo Urioste shared his time and wisdom with us. We love our cover which was painted by Clif Tinker. Finally our thanks go out to Sister Joyce Blum for living the Gospel, and the willingness and patience to share her story with us.

Donations for the Shelby County Catholic Church's
Central American project can be sent to:

St. Michael's Catholic Church
Central America Project
1912 18th St.
Harlan, IA 51537

To order additional copies of this book, please contact:
Patricia Graeve Michels
1325 Elmwood Rd
Panama, IA 51562-6604
e-mail: **jpmichelsfarm@gmail.com**

1 copy: $10.00 + $3.00 S&H / *Payable to:* Sister Joyce Blum Book

Quantity discounts available upon request.

Table of Contents

Foreword

In 1960, Pope John XXIII invited U.S. Religious Congregations of women and men to send members of their communities to Latin America within the next ten years. In response, the Franciscan Sisters of Perpetual Adoration (FSPA) sent three of our sisters to Santa Anna, El Salvador in 1962 to work with Maryknoll ministry initiatives. A year later, Sister Joyce Blum volunteered to minister in El Salvador.

After leaving the U.S. in 1963, Sister Joyce ministered in parishes through the Santa Anna region as an adult educator. Living from her missionary heart and spirit, Sister Joyce served with and for the people of El Salvador for thirteen years. She actively embraced the five strategic principles formulated by the FSPA mission direction:

- work where the needs are greatest and where the influence will be the greatest
- promote dialogue as the basis for Christian life and love
- be mindful of the testimony of poverty in the missionary life
- promote family life and education; help train leaders and catechists in order to form committed Christians, and
- make positive efforts to be replaced eventually by nationals (laity) in the work.

From the past, present and into the future, Sister Joyce's mission heart never misses the opportunity to be of Christian service. Her love and compassion especially for the marginalized is core to Sister Joyce. Her ministry as a member of the Shelby County Six Catholic Parish team to the people of Central America is an active extension of her heart and previous mission experience. It is who she is!

~ *Suzanne Rubenbauer, FSPA*

CHAPTER ONE

Growing Up

Today

San Pedro is located in the department of La Paz, El Salvador. The road into town is narrow and winding, but not terrible as roads can sometimes be in Central America. Green, forested country lines both sides of the road which leads up into the highlands of west central El Salvador. The highlands are not really mountains by our standards, but the land is much too high and steep for the tractors we use back in Iowa. The people here still plant corn and beans in the hills, but, of course only by hand.

Ten or fifteen kilometers farther up the road there is a small village with a lovely white Catholic church. It stands at the highest point of this area and overlooks an expansive wooded valley with villages mixed in here and there. If you come around dusk as we had, the western-facing view will provide one of the most spectacular sunsets you will ever see.

San Pedro itself is a fair-sized town, not big enough to be called a city but big enough to be the main market town in the region and have a large Catholic church. We were visiting Monsignor Carpio, the pastor of the church, and he was giving us a tour. Our group also included Jimmy, a seminarian who lived in the rectory, John, who works for Caritas[1] , Father Jose Reynaldo Hernadez, our guide, four of us[2] from Shelby County, Iowa, and of course Sister Joyce Blum, FSPA.[3] Before Vatican II, she was known as Sister Germaine. In El Salvador, she was called Hermana Yoece (Sister Joyce) or Madre Alegria, (Mother of Joy) as named by a local bishop. Today she is called Sister Joyce or just Joyce. She has picked up more than one name because she has served her Franciscan order in many places for over fifty years.

---

[1] Caritas is the equivalent of Catholic Charities in the United States
[2] Patricia Graeve Michels, Tim Sullivan, Charlotte Willenborg and photographer Pat Sullivan
[3] Franciscan Sisters of Perpetual Adoration

If you had passed our group that day, you would have noticed most of us had gentle smiles on our faces and we all were waiting patiently as Sister Joyce was once again visiting with another group of complete strangers. This time it looked like a family of four generations—a great grandma, a grandma, a mom and a daughter. I suspect in the five minutes they visited with Sister, she learned all their names, where they lived, what they were doing that day and pretty much everything else about their lives. It was clear everyone was enjoying the conversation.

We were always patiently waiting for Sister as she visited with the local Salvadorans or people of any other nation for that matter. It was a common occurrence we had kidded Sister about, so a couple of days later when she was visiting with a man near his home, we were taking bets to see if she was going to ask him to invite us into his home. Soon, she turned to us with a sheepish grin and said, "We are going to visit his home now." She followed up with, "He invited us."

The four of us from Iowa, five with Sister Joyce, were on a kind of pilgrimage. Our journey was to understand and maybe more truthfully experience this woman so full of life, joy and love of people. What inspires a woman at eighteen to leave her beloved family and safe home in Iowa, join a community of women and ultimately, live in a difficult, remote, hot, dusty, primitive country often in dangerous circumstances? How could she find such joy and beauty in poor rural people four thousand miles from her home?

Joyce spent over thirteen years in El Salvador, so this is where we begin our journey. But, of course the story of Joyce Blum started in Iowa.

1936-1962

Shelby County is located in the rolling hills of western Iowa. Before the settlers moved in it was mostly tall grass prairie. In fact, at one time there were 240 million acres of what Europeans called the "inland sea." Prairie grass sends down its roots first, up to eleven feet.[1] After the root system is well-developed, the grass grows tall, rising up from the soil. When the Germans arrived around 1851, they settled the hills that would become western Shelby County, turned the land with the iron plow, and found some of the deepest and most fertile topsoil in the world. It was a good place to build a home, live, and put down roots just as the tall grass had done. By 1900 over 17,000 people lived in Shelby County and most of the prairie was replaced with crops of corn, wheat, oats, and pasture for cattle. By the 1920's the landscape was covered with small self-sufficient farmsteads. Most farms grew several types of grain using horse-drawn equipment, raised cattle, pigs, chickens, a few milk cows and a huge garden. The people lived off the land; it was labor intensive, and the size of the families matched the need for labor.

The settlers brought their religion with them, including the priests and sisters of the Catholic Church. The towns of Defiance, Earling, Panama, Portsmouth, and Westphalia had been established and each came with a Catholic church to serve the almost exclusively German Catholic people of the area. It was in this special place that Chris Blum the youngest of sixteen children began his courtship of Nora Pauley. Both Chris and Nora attended school for three or four years. Chris was a tall thin teenager with his hair parted down the middle when he showed up on Nora's doorstep for the first time. He was quiet and respectful, always waiting his turn to speak. Nora made it very clear to Chris from the start; if he was interested in her he would have to wait because she needed to take care of her elderly father first. But Chris was a patient fellow and on September 28, 1926, they were married.

Chris and Nora were renting a farm from Chris's grandfather when they started their family together. Soon they began the process of buying their own 240 acre farm in the rolling hills about a mile and a half west of Panama. Joyce was the middle child of eleven, born in 1936. By the time she came along Joyce already had three older brothers and two sisters. There was no going to the hospital when the children were born; the doctor would show up at the house and a few hours later they would have another baby brother or sister. Joyce always wondered how the doctor fit that baby in his little black bag that he always carried. Her earliest memories are of being a daddy's girl. Charley, her immediate older brother, had some health issues in his early years and took most of their mother's attention, so Joyce spent a lot of time with her father. In retrospect, Joyce always thought the 'daddy's little girl syndrome' created an inner power in her that flowed from the strong paternal figure.

Joyce has nothing but fond memories of both her parents. Her dad was a tall stately man, quiet but with a good sense of humor, and great with the kids. He was a hard worker. His large hands came in handy around the farm, and Joyce inherited both traits from him. Her mother was also a hard worker. Both parents were deeply religious.

Joyce told a story about her mom and her apron that gives a good picture of their farm life.

Mom and Her Apron

"My mother wore the apron all the time while at home. This was her work uniform and was with her each day. I could make an apron as well as other straight seams on our old foot pumped Singer sewing machine.

In some of my earliest memories, it is the magic apron that I smile about. It was often made out of those floral "Mother's Best" flour sacks. Yes, there was a bib and certainly two pockets, and I mean BIG pockets.

Another magical element of the apron was its many uses. My mother would be back in the woods looking for apples. She had no need for a basket or a pail because mother would just fold up her apron, and in would go the apples.

She also used her apron to gather up loose chicks, or when out in the garden; she would use the apron to carry a bunch of freshly picked peas to shell for supper. Can you see mother standing at the clothes line with the apron folded neatly upward and filled with clothes pins?

Have you ever seen such a utilitarian piece of clothing? To be sure when the apron was seen worn inside out it meant my mom was on her way to a more 'dirty' job, such as feeding the cows, or going to the garden. That way if a salesman happened along; mom would just turn the apron back to its clean pretty side out and so be fittingly presented to take care of visitors.

Mom's work varied. There would be the times mom wiped away a tear from some child's eye, pulled pans of hot bread from the cob kitchen stove or even shooed chickens out of the house yard.

Sitting on the front steps with my little sisters, I can still see my mother coming from the chicken barn with an apron full of eggs. Then there was the time the same apron provided protection from some feisty roosters who were intimidating my little sister. You know it seemed that the roosters could sense a child's fear and would come running straight at a little one with flapping wings.

Our long farm lane allowed mom to see any car coming, and time to dust off a chair, a dresser, and to toss the apron in a secret location as she stood all prim and pretty to converse with a sales person.

The apron never went to town, and certainly never went to church… the apron was 'home-made' to save the dress underneath."

The Blum's life on the farm was full of hard work and lots of fun. There was no electricity until Joyce was in high school which meant no television, computers, or any kind of electric appliance. There was no indoor plumbing either, just an outhouse which the boys moved every so often. Since Joyce spent the early part of her life without electricity and indoor plumbing, it made her transition to similar circumstances later in El Salvador much easier.

As soon as you were able, you had chores to do. One of the first jobs Joyce ever had was to watch the cow tank fill, and shut off the water before it overflowed. All summer was spent getting ready for winter. They canned jars of beans, meat, carrots, apple sauce, and other fruits and vegetables which were stored in the cellar to eat during the winter months. Potatoes were stored in a bin, and carrots lasted a long time stored in sand in the cellar. They milked their own cows, which the girls did when the boys were thrashing oats in the summer or bringing in the harvest in the fall. They had a special milking stool of their own patent, and the cows were usually quite tame, but occasionally one would kick the milk bucket. Whenever this happened, it took a couple of days before they could work up the nerve to milk again. If the cow kicked you instead of the bucket, she could do real damage. Of course, the milking was all done by hand so the Blum girls' forearms were stronger than those of the town boys.

By the time Joyce was fifteen years old, God had given her another brother and four more sisters. Now she had six sisters and four brothers, and she loved them all.

The Blum girls did not get dolls or store-bought toys, nor did they get paid or have allowances. But very early her mother let her care for her baby brothers and sisters, and it made her happier than any doll could have. During the summer, as soon as the little ones were off to slumberland, Joyce would run out to the orchard with the older kids. They had a log which they pretended was a house. It had sleeping quarters and other rooms. They spent a lot of time there, canning plums

The Chris and Nora Blum family—1951

and rhubarb in old jars, and baking mud pies, bread and cookies. Their dad always said they had to eat what they made, but somehow they managed to see that the mud pies were disposed of in some other way. They had a lot of chickens, and one day they decided eggs would be good whipped with the mud solution. When their mom came to do chicken chores, they were caught red-handed. The punishment must have been severe because they never talked about it and never did it again. The few toys they had they made themselves in their dad's garage. Most of the time they even remembered to put the tools back. Whatever they were doing, as soon as the little kids would cry out back at the house, her mom would call, and Joyce would dash back in to be a good little "mother" again.

As the family grew, so did the Blum's farm. They added two other farms in addition to the home place so there was always plenty of work to go around. The girls took their turn in the hay, corn, and grain fields and tried to keep up with the boys. They all came home with great farmer tans. In her late teens Joyce would often drive the tractor, but for many years the family relied on their farm animals. They had two mules named Jack and Jenny, and several work horses including

Jerry and Sam. Everyone's favorite was the pony named Prince, who entertained the Blum kids for many years.

The pony, Prince, with Charley, Judy and Audrey

The Blum family knew how to have fun. There were a couple of tire swings on the side of the house, and even though the ropes were weathered rotten and the tires worn, they had great fun there. One day Joyce and one of her sisters decided to see who could stay on the longest without getting dizzy. Joyce, being very charitable, allowed her sister to be spun first. Around and around she went until she began to turn colors and vomit, with Joyce laughing her lungs out the whole time. That was enough of that and of course Joyce won!

"Kick the Can" was one of their most beloved games. Joyce's sister Alice tells a story about the time Joyce got her front tooth broken off. According to Alice, to this day, Joyce blames her cousin Russell for running the wrong way around the house.

They were a sort of sports franchise in their own right. From the time they were little their dad and the older kids had taught everyone how to bat and catch. When you have that many competitive kids around (Plus, most of the neighbors had equally large families), it was a ball game just waiting to happen. Summer evenings after supper the neighborhood kids would come over for a softball game. They would choose sides and play until dark. The post-game treat was egg beer, a recipe consisting of raw beaten eggs, water, vanilla, and sugar.

Basketball was the Blum family's best game. All the neighbors said the Blums were a basketball-playing family and Joyce reinforced this by getting on the All County Basketball team. For the most part they were a tall group and their dad often played at home with them. Joyce loved her dad's wonderful spirit; whenever anyone got hurt or would come with a scratch, he would say, "Oh, don't let a little thing like that bother."

Joyce in her high school
basketball uniform

The Blum kids also had fun at playing church. Skylark candies were the communion. The girls knew all the Latin Mass prayers just like the boys. Of course in the Blum children's church the girls could not only be altar servers but also priests. At that time women could do neither, though now they can at least be altar servers in most places. The Catholic faith was a major part of their lives. Joyce's early faith experience was church, family prayer, often daily Mass, and always Sunday Mass with the whole family. The Blum family had its own pew at St. Mary's Church in Panama and filled it to overflowing. There were morning and evening prayers at home and a prayer of thanksgiving before every meal. During Lent all the children would kneel around their dad, with the youngest child in his lap, as he led the whole family in the rosary.

All the kids went to St. Mary's Catholic School where a more formal religious formation took place. Joyce received Holy Communion in the second grade with careful preparation led by the Benedictine sisters and Monsignor

M. B. Schiltz. Joyce remembers sitting on the cob bin[4] as her mother asked her questions from the catechism. She knew it so well; she could tell if her mom skipped a question.

In the fourth grade Solemn Communion was made, baptismal vows were renewed, and in the celebration's procession Joyce was privileged to help crown Mary, the Queen of May. Dressed in white, Joyce marched in all the processions during grade school including the procession where she and three friends carried the Blessed Lady. The best scholars in her class were chosen, and since they only had a class of twenty-five, the competition was not so great. They did have a hard time finding someone to match her up with that was close to her height.

In eighth grade Joyce's class was confirmed by Bishop Arkfeld of Papua New Guinea. The Bishop, who grew up in Shelby County, came back every three or four years to do confirmation. By this time Joyce had already decided she wanted to become a sister.

Getting to school could be a challenge. There were no school buses and it was too far to walk. Usually they carpooled with the neighbors in a Model A Ford. Imagine a driver and nine kids squeezed into the car. In the spring when the ground thawed and the rains came, the roads were impassable with the Ford. The only thing that could move through the deep mud was a horse drawn wagon. It had side walls and very high, thin wheels. The kids sat on benches in the back of the wagon with books, lunch bags, and sufficient clothes to get them to school. The wheels could sink two feet into the mud and the kids wondered how they could possibly make it up and over the hills without sliding into the ditches.

High school seemed like there was always something going on. Joyce's memories from her freshman year are mostly about initiation rituals led by the seniors, minor abuses like bowing to the seniors and doing a week of penance. The sophomore year brought festivals, operettas, and plays. The junior and senior years were filled with dances, banquets, proms, and a skip day to Nebraska. Joyce was always active in clubs; she was president of the Sodality, class officer, captain of the Sports Club, a member of the St. Cecilia's Glee Club, and on the staff of the school paper.

Joyce's sister, Alice, commented, "Sister was a perfect child. Mom said so too. She was good." The closest thing to a ruffled Joyce happened in the summer after her senior year. Joyce went to Mass and Communion every morning. Her mom insisted on calling Joyce in the morning rather than giving her the alarm clock. One morning Joyce was just lying in bed waiting to be called. When she finally got up, she saw that it was already 7:00 and she could not make it the two miles to church on time. Joyce must have shown her feelings at some point because her mom commented with a

---

[4] A cob bin is a storage bin for corn cobs which they used to cook with.

smile, saying "Oh, "Totie" is angry at me because I let her sleep." Later Joyce would pray, "Dear God, forgive me for being cross with her sometimes and the rest of the family. How could one be angry at such a wonderful person?"

Somehow Joyce knew from a young age she wanted to be a religious sister. It was probably the influence of the Benedictine sisters. Joyce was not really aware of it at the time, but Shelby County had a tremendous track record for supplying priests, sisters, and brothers for the Catholic Church. The small town of Westphalia, which in 1940 only had 126 people,[2] has sent 72 young women to join religious orders over the years.[3] The small communities that surround the county seat of Harlan, (Defiance, Earling, Panama, Portsmouth, and Westphalia) sent 164 sisters, 56 priests, and two brothers to a variety of religious orders throughout their history.[4,5,6,7]

In the 1940's when Joyce was growing up, most people lived on farms. For example, in 1940 Harlan was the largest town in Shelby County with about 3,700 people. The county had around 15,942 people. Now Harlan has about 5,100 people and the county 12,000.[8] Today there are fewer farms with smaller families and the population is aging. Younger people are often moving away to cities. When Joyce was growing up, the families were large; not all of the kids could stay and become farmers. It was kind of expected that one or two of your fifteen kids would join a religious order.

Not only did Shelby County provide a large number of religious vocations, but there were several religious who spent most of their working lives as missionaries. Probably the most well-known was Archbishop Leo Arkfeld from Panama, who served in Papua New Guinea. He was the youngest bishop in the world in 1943 when he was appointed at age thirty-six. That was five years after the Japanese murdered his immediate predecessor Bishop Joseph Lorks, SVD along with 38 priests, brothers, and sisters.[9]

Because of the difficulty of reaching the people Archbishop Arkfeld served, he began flying into the remote villages, earning him the nicknames: the "Flying Priest" and later the "Flying Bishop." He was a practical missionary, very down to earth.[9] Many of the missionaries that have come out of Shelby County with their farm backgrounds were very practical and hard-working people.

Other Catholic missionaries from Shelby County include Father Vincent Ohlinger, SVD from Panama, who also served in Papua New Guinea. From Westphalia, there were Father Bernard Zimmerman, SJ, who served in British Honduras or what is now called Belize, and Father Anthony Zimmerman, SVD served in Japan.

Many of the missionaries of this time period lived through wars or revolutions. Sister M. Corsina, FSPA from Westphalia served in China during World War II. In 1938 Sister Corsina and the other sisters who worked in an orphanage had to evacuate the city with the children because of extensive bombing by the Japanese. Sister Corsina died of Dengue fever and was buried in Wuchang, China. Whenever sisters volunteered to go on mission they were told not to expect to return to the United States. It was a lifetime commitment.

Father Paul Koch was in a class behind Joyce at St. Mary's Catholic School in Panama. Father Paul served as a priest for the Diocese of Des Moines. He had an opportunity to volunteer for missionary work for the same reason Joyce had. In 1961 Pope John XXIII requested religious orders in the United States to send 10% of their members to Latin America to support the Church's work there. Father Paul spent forty years in Bolivia and has just recently come home to serve the growing Latino population in Iowa. Bolivia went through many of the same struggles as El Salvador. His missionary story could also teach us a great deal about the realities of life in Latin America. Joyce was indeed joining in a great tradition of religious involvement from Shelby County, Iowa.

The summer of 1954 was unlike any other summer in Joyce's young life. She knew she wanted to be a sister but did not have a clue as to which order she wanted to join. Joyce had visited the Benedictines in Kansas during her senior year of school. These were the same nuns who taught at St. Mary's and had such a great influence on Joyce. They offered one scholarship a year to a graduate of St. Mary's. In Joyce's senior year they were originally going to give it to a good friend of Joyce's, but her friend broke the skip day rules, so the sisters withdrew the offer. Joyce was their backup choice, but she never felt comfortable accepting what should have been her friend's scholarship. The decision of which order to join was dropped for the time being and Joyce kept her feelings to herself. Later some of her sister friends would tease her about being "a righteous stoic."

In June, Joyce and her mom took the train to Milwaukee to a reception for a cousin in the Franciscan Order of Lake Drive. That was their excuse for going, but really Joyce was continuing her search and met with the Mother General while they were there. They had a great visit, but the Spirit did not move her in that direction. She was already growing weary and frustrated with a search that just could not satisfy that unknown "something."

In July, Joyce's sister Virginia accompanied her to visit Sister Ann Marie, the vocation director at St. Rose's Convent with the Franciscan Sisters of Perpetual Adoration in La Crosse, Wisconsin. They visited the convent, the Villa (sisters' retirement home), and took in the local sites. La Crosse is located on the Mississippi River, and Joyce was inspired by the beauty of the setting. On the way home she told her sister that this was where she wanted to go. No one was pushing her to go to La Crosse, but she was sure that was where God wanted her. Back at home, her mom made her wait two weeks to send in her application, thinking that perhaps the novelty would wear off, but Joyce had no doubts. Soon she was packing her bags.

There was a long list of things to bring: funny shoes, black stockings, black dresses, and undergarments. Joyce's mother made all of their clothes out of feed sacks and did not feel she was a good enough seamstress to sew convent clothes, so she hired a woman from Westphalia to sew them for her. The most amazing piece was a housecoat; Joyce had never heard of such a garment before.

It was a long drive from Panama, Iowa, to La Crosse, Wisconsin on that day in August of 1954 when Chris and Nora Blum gave their daughter back to God to serve the People. It was both a sad and joyous day. Three of Chris's sisters had joined the Milwaukee Franciscans years ago, so they were familiar with religious life. Nora had confessed to Joyce she had also wanted to be a sister but stayed home to take care of her ailing father instead. St. Rose's Convent was located in the countryside outside of La Crosse. Chris and Nora stayed for a few days as Joyce became familiar with the convent. They left Joyce with the sister in charge, Sr. Charlotte. She was an older nun so Chris and Nora felt comfortable leaving their Joyce in her hands. There were 52 other young women who initially joined Joyce's class that August.

Joyce had no time to feel lonely. She was busy marking clothes and organizing. Each student was given a number (Joyce's was 28) and it went on every piece of clothing. It was easy for her to mix in, get started on college, do chores, meet the Sisters and her classmates, and begin a new life inside the walls of the convent. Joyce said, "I was not doing anything new because I came from a community lifestyle, with a family of six sisters and four brothers, where everyone helped each other, played and prayed together."

Though there were similarities to her former life, there were also adjustments to make. For example, Joyce's home on the farm had no indoor plumbing, so at the convent she enjoyed the convenience it provided. Rather more difficult to adjust to were the different backgrounds most of her classmates came from. The vast majority of the girls came from families who lived in the city, were more affluent, or had attended larger high schools with more resources. She always felt like the less-sophisticated girl from the farm. Still, most of the changes brought only joy into Joyce's life. She loved the silence, prayer time, and the convent classes. Indeed she was truly following in the footsteps of Saint Francis and Saint Claire of Assisi.

Before Joyce knew it, her first year of classes was over, and it was time for their summer break. Joyce spent five days visiting family and friends back in Iowa. The rest of the summer was spent at the Villa, taking a speech class, working in the garden, going for walks in the bluffs, and even cleaning a chicken or two. It is easy to imagine Joyce excelling at that job. By the time August rolled around, she was ready to be back at the convent. She missed the other sisters and the Adoration Chapel.

They had a ten day retreat before starting back to classes. Joyce loved the time she got to spend alone with Jesus and his mother Mary. Novitiate days were here, and it was a special time. They had walks, picnics, and so many little fun-packed occasions. And some days, in the midst of it all, their mistress would produce a box of candy as if by magic. From the exclamations of ooh's and ah's, you would think they never got candy. It was the unexpectedness which caused the outbursts. Reflecting on those happy times, you could not find one thing which was outstanding, yet Joyce had such a feeling of peace. The simplicity of everything they did is what lent such charm to their lives.

The second year the focus was primarily on formation. In the third and fourth years Joyce did a combination of teaching in rural Iowa schools and taking classes. The fifth year was an intense year of prayer and school to finish up education classes. Through it all, the saying "Fall in love with Christ" was heard over and over, and Joyce was firmly convinced that is what she was there for. It all led to perpetual vows and a life where the only desire was to go and do as God called her.

Today most religious sisters have their college degree before they begin formation in an order, but when Joyce joined, college and formation were blended together in the overall formation package. Joyce would be the first in her family to get a college degree. It took six years to not only get her degree but to progress through all the different levels of vows. It was hard work but also mostly great fun for Joyce. How privileged Joyce felt to have such good teachers and so many inspiring theology classes! Before entering the convent, life around her seemed so complex- money, noise, food, or some kind of activity was needed to make one feel happy. But now Joyce felt that the less she had, the happier she was. How slow we are sometimes to appreciate the simple things that come from God.

The time for perpetual vows had come. Imagine the excitement of a bride on her wedding day! This is the excitement Joyce felt, for she was to be wed to Christ. A few years after Joyce took her perpetual vows she would journal:

Vows....

"Receive me, O Lord according to thy word and I shall live. Let it not be confounded in my expectations." As you sang these simple words, not so many years ago, and as you asked to be admitted to the profession of simple vows, you were totally unaware of what the future had in store for you. You were aware of the fact that you wanted to give yourself completely to God, according to His word, whether that be by working with His poor in China, in the first grade class room, in the kitchen, in the music room or whether you were sick or well.

"I thank the Holy Spirit for loving me and guiding me to Christ... I thank Christ for accepting me and giving me so many good Sisters. May I live always as a worthy spouse of Him whom the angels serve."

With her perpetual vows in place, Joyce was now Sister Joyce Blum, FSPA, and was ready to put her calling into practice. She was privileged to get a taste of what she thought missionary work would be like when she did her practice teaching in Lansing, Iowa, and she knew she would like it. Joyce had already decided she was either going to be a missionary or work in one of their orphanages.

With Pope John XXIII's call to send missionaries to Latin America, it was easy to decide which way she would go. She recognized there were so many souls just waiting to hear about God, and she was ready to give and give until she could not give anymore. She knew she chose a life of sacrifice and she would follow her Master to Calvary, carrying her cross beside Him. She also realized as a woman who loved babies, she was sacrificing the opportunity for motherhood as she reflected in this journal entry:

Motherhood

When I answered the Franciscan vocation in 1954 with the FSPAs in La Crosse, I knew that I would never be privileged to shelter another human being within my own body. It was a gift freely given.

In 1962 the Franciscans from La Crosse sent three sisters to start a school in Santa Ana, El Salvador, and in 1963 Sister Joyce Blum was sent to serve in their new school.

CHAPTER TWO

El Salvador

Today

It has been over thirty-five years since Joyce left El Salvador and not once in those thirty-five years has she returned to the land and people that she has grown to love. Today, December 31, 2013, as we worked our way through customs, her joy and excitement were evident as she spoke to every El Salvadorian she came within arms-length of. It was 85 degrees and sunny when we arrived.

San Salvador is the largest city in El Salvador, with a population of close to two million people. It is a thriving and busy city, and with the exception of the poor barrio neighborhoods, it could have been Omaha, Nebraska. El Salvador is a country sandwiched between Guatemala, Honduras, and the Pacific Ocean. It has the most people per square kilometer and is the most urban of all countries in Central America. The Pacific coast of El Salvador has beautiful white beaches and what some say are the best surfing waves in Central America. As you move away from the coast, fields of sugar cane dominate the lowlands; mountains and river valleys make up the rest of El Salvador. The country has twenty volcanoes, and as a matter of fact, the volcano, Chaparrastique, near San Miguel, erupted two days before we arrived.

We were met at the airport by Father Jose Reynaldo Hernadez and his friend, Cesar. We were also surprised to see Bishop Bolaños at the airport. Father Jose had mentioned to the bishop that morning that we were coming to El Salvador, and he volunteered to drive us to where we would be staying. Sister Joyce and the bishop visited as we traveled from the airport. Sister, who is never bashful, asked the bishop about the possibility of bringing Salvadoran Sisters to Iowa, since the state has quite a large population of Central American immigrants. Because of the civil war in El Salvador and the desire to build a better life, many Salvadorans have migrated to the United States. After Sister's frank conversation with the bishop, she smiled and said, "We could use more bishops like him, bishops with humility who listen and are willing to speak candidly. Now that's transparency."

El Salvador

Central America

(Maps reprinted with permission.)

After the bishop dropped us off at our temporary home, Father Jose took us to his family's house where his mother had prepared delicious tamales for us. The warm welcome by the Bishop and Father Jose and his family were just the first instances of the hospitality we received throughout our trip in El Salvador. It's easy to understand why, when sister came here thirty-five years ago, she immediately felt like she was back with family in Shelby County.

Father Jose, his parents and our group.

1963-1965

The climate in San Salvador in 1963 was nothing like La Crosse, Wisconsin. In the full habit of the Franciscan Sisters, Joyce was sweating before she made it out of the airport. The customs officers took their time as they went through Joyce's suitcases. She had quite a load because she wasn't planning on leaving anytime soon. They searched through every piece of clothing, books, pens, and rosaries that she had packed. Naturally Sister offered them one of the rosaries made by her father, and they took the brightest colored ones they could find. Any small discomfort Joyce may have felt from the heat was far outweighed by the excitement she felt at her first missionary assignment.

Three of her Franciscan Sisters picked her up at the airport. She was on her way to Santa Ana. The Maryknolls[5] had built a school in the parish of Madre del Salvador, and the Franciscan Sisters were going to run it. The parish hall, school, rectory, and convent were all located in the very poor barrio of San Raphael, which was on the edge of Santa Ana. The school was built on the site of an old garbage dump with train tracks running right through it. It would not be the last time Joyce would live and work on an abandoned garbage pit. It says something about our world that the poorest of the poor seem to inherit the dumps of the rich. These poverty-stricken people were the ones Joyce came to serve. Later, Joyce would journal about her first impressions:

Born Free

As a Franciscan, I belong to this Church, I find my deepest connectedness with the poor. How else can one sit under the stars each evening listening to the silence of the Almighty? I am again aware of dirt, ground level realities just up the road being a garbage dump. How much garbage production is connected to the lives of the people? Have you thought that it is the powerful that take over the territory of the poor by dumping their garbage in the middle of where the poor live?

Today, Santa Ana is the second-largest city in El Salvador. It is located in the far north central part of the country, closer to Guatemala than the capital city of San

---

[5]An American Catholic religious order that reaches out to the most marginalized in the world.

Salvador. The main businesses and the few wealthy land owners lived in the center of the city with its paved roads. However, the majority of the city's population lived on the edges of the community where the dirt roads turned to mud in the rainy season. It was a hard life with very few people having what we would call a real job. Most found work in construction, doing carpentry, or buying and selling whatever they could. But they did work, and November through January with their whole families in tow, would leave their homes every day and go to the hillsides to pick coffee, as Santa Ana lies in the heart of coffee country. The coffee industry, along with the wealthy elite landowners, dominated El Salvador politics and society.

The history of El Salvador is a history of struggle for the peasant population. In 1524 the Spaniard Pedro de Alvarado came down from Mexico and crushed the native opposition of the area and reduced them to vassals of the crown.[1] The early 1800's brought independence from Spain and a series of attempts to unite the Central American countries into a single state.

It was a turbulent time and through it all, the peasants served a ruling class. For centuries the peasants survived with a multi-crop system which they produced on small plots of land, working for the landowners on their larger farms. But this changed in the 1860's when the landowners, led by Gerardo Barrios, decided to join other Central American countries in the mass production of coffee.

Coffee was a cash crop that caused an economic upheaval everywhere it was grown. Small farmers could not eat coffee; it is an export crop for profit only. This was fine for the landowners but of little value to the peasants who did not have the land or resources to export. Before the age of coffee, El Salvador had a balanced economy of grain, fruit, and other crops. Over the next fifty years the coffee market expanded as well as the land owned by the large coffee producers. This additional land was taken from the small plots of land the peasants owned. "If a small landholder refused to sell, the rich man or the 'coffee man,' went to the local or department camandante" and forced the small landholder to sell.[2] By the 1920's coffee had created a class of extreme wealth consisting of around twenty families that owned most of the land and controlled the politics of the country. The rest of the population sank ever further into peonage.

Of course there were good masters and bad masters, but in general it seems their lives working for the coffee masters were not enviable in the least. One description says, "The owner was a rude and authoritarian man who made his peasants' families work all week for an insignificant salary and took from their pay at the end of the week a peso from each for the rent of the hovel where they lived. The rest of the salary was not given in real money but tokens which could only be used to buy food, clothing, medicines, and trinkets from the wife of the master."[3]

Coffee is a flowering plant growing five to eight feet high depending on the variety. The berries turn a bright red when ripe, usually in December through

January. Because all the berries on a single plant do not ripen at the same time, the families Joyce served would pick coffee three or even four times from a single plant. The best coffee grows at higher altitudes and on fairly steep hills. During coffee season, entire families would hike up into the hills and fill buckets with coffee berries, later pouring the buckets into large canvas bags. They were paid by the bucketful. It was heavy work and the pay was minimal, at best.

Many of the people also worked in the processing of coffee. It was a big business, with processing centers and storage systems as large as those used in the United States for corn and beans. The first processing step removes the red pulp of the berry, exposing two beans that are soaked in water and then dried. Finally, a thin shell is removed from the beans and then they are roasted. The final quality of the coffee's taste depends on each of these steps, and there is a wide range of quality available. The best coffee is shipped out of the country, and only the poorest quality is used locally.

The lives of the people revolved around the coffee crop. The schools closed November through January so that families could go pick coffee together. Joyce was shocked by the disparity between peoples' poverty surrounded by rich coffee plantations and huge coffee processing facilities.

It took time to get used to the hot, dry, and dusty climate. In a few months she would have to adjust to the humid rainy season.

The convent where the sisters lived was very modern both by El Salvador's and by Joyce's standards. It had running water and electricity, but of course no hot water. Older buildings had no windows, and more modern block buildings, like the convent, had bars on the windows.

Most of the food was bought in the local markets with their friend and helper Sofia. These were open air markets where the people sold their homegrown produce and vegetables, and where butchered meat hung from the stalls. Joyce enjoyed the simple food and soon learned what was safe or not safe to eat. For example, the homemade cheese they aged by hanging it in a tree was off limits because of all the flies that swarmed the cheese. Sofia also taught her to only buy live chickens and let them run for a few days in the yard. If they were still alive after a couple of days, they were safe to eat. She said never buy ground up meat because you might find some surprises. There were a couple of small family stores that sold groceries like boxed cereal, but the sisters had to check the cereal closely for bugs. Wormy apples were a rare treat, but the fruit of choice was mangos. Papayas were also very common, but it took Joyce a while to appreciate their taste. People were buying and selling everywhere. Many of the street corners had a woman with a foot-pumped sewing machine making clothes. You could not buy clothes in a store in the poor barrio neighborhoods; everything was made in homes or by these women on the street corners.

Joyce arrived in Santa Ana early in the year of 1963. The school would not open until the fall of that year so Joyce's first job was to learn the language and get to know the people she was there to serve. What a shock to be a straight-A Spanish student in school but to, not in the least, be able to follow a conversation now that she was in Spanish-speaking El Salvador. A Spanish dictionary accompanied her everywhere. Smiles and hugs dominated the conversations with occasional words; there was no such thing as a complete, much less a correct, sentence. But none of this was a problem for Joyce. She loved these simple people from the first day. As hard as their lives were, they were a welcoming, friendly people that reminded her of her small-town community back in Panama, Iowa.

One thing that was different from the German farmers back home was the way the Salvadorans expressed their feelings. In El Salvador Joyce learned to share her feelings, hugs, and kisses. They loved to have this beautiful, loving North American sister come visit their homes.

Most of the homes were simple mud and bamboo shacks or "mesons" as they were called in this San Raphael barrio. Just imagine this tall, smiling, white woman in an all-white habit walking up the dirt street of the barrio as she approached your simple meson. The bottom of her habit was coated with dust and dirt and she had to bend way over to make it inside because the local people were considerably shorter than Joyce. She would sit on a home-made stool and could not stand up straight because the ceilings were so low. She could only speak a broken kind of Spanish, but it did not bother her or the family because they were happy to have her as a guest.

Joyce remembers a visit to an old woman's home in which upon entering the house and letting her eyes adjust to the darkness, she noticed a little wooden box stored on a tree limb. The woman explained that she was old and would die soon, and this was her casket. Joyce had no words with which to respond, just a look of love, and a hug. Joyce loved the humility of the families;

they truly lived the communion prayer, "Lord I am not worthy that you should enter under my roof."

Joyce often visited the local hospital which was little more than a large dorm. It was hot in the hospital with lots of yelling and crying. Sometimes they would have three patients to a bed. If someone died they were buried within twenty-four hours because of the heat. The family would put the body in a simple wooden casket or wrap it in a sheet and carry it through the barrio to the cemetery. A large crowd of family and friends would follow. Joyce thought it an amazing sight the first time she saw a funeral procession.

They celebrated Mass every morning. Some of the sisters were great musicians, so singing was an important part of Mass. On weekends the people would bring in local instruments and the Masses would come to life. Joyce would return often to the same streets and homes in an effort to build relationships. She would visit for a short time, encourage the family to sign their children up for catechism classes or for school in the fall, and maybe drop off a picture of Jesus. Her walks through the streets were Joyce's prime time to learn. She absorbed whatever the people could teach her about language, simple joyful living, and the hard realities of their lives.

When Joyce began to teach catechism classes, the Maryknoll Father suggested that she also teach English. The Father had contacts in the wealthier parts of Santa Ana and she was soon being paid to teach English to wealthy Salvadoran women. She had a set schedule for classes, and the women paid from the time the class was scheduled to start whether they showed up on time or not. They were often late - sometimes they were only there for five minutes of the class time - but they always paid for an hour and never got upset. The priests and sisters took it upon themselves to teach the people the idea of timeliness. The North American priests' Masses always started on time and the sisters' classes always started on time, but to the Salvadorans a watch was only an accessory. Joyce and the other sisters got to know these women well and soon they were invited to use their homes along Lake Coatepeque for a get-away. The sisters would occasionally have retreat days there.

One of Joyce's most vivid memories of her first year was the assassination of President John F. Kennedy in Dallas on November 22, 1963. Transistor radios were common and the means from which most people got their news. The "Voice of America" was broadcasted into El Salvador in both English and Spanish. They provided coverage on all major news stories like the Cuba Missile Crisis and Neil Armstrong's walk on the moon. Joyce remembers huddling around the radio with her fellow Franciscans and shedding more than a few tears as they waited for the ultimate news that President Kennedy was dead.

Another significant event that happened in the lives of sisters was that they were given the option of not wearing traditional habits. For Joyce's small community in El Salvador it was fairly easy to come to consensus on what they were going to wear. In the United States it was much more difficult because there were huge numbers of sisters to work with.

The change did bring a couple unintended outcomes. For example, soon after the change, one of the sisters took some visitors on a tour of the local markets that lasted most of the day. She came back to the convent with terrible sunburn on her forehead; after all it had not seen sunlight in many years. For Joyce a different problem was caused by the habit change: it meant she would need to buy new shoes, which was easier said than done. Joyce's feet were rather large in comparison to the feet of Salvadoran women. In fact, her shoe size in the Salvadoran scale was about a 42, (a women's size 10 in the U.S.) Believe it or not she did find shoes her size, but said, "They fit my head better than my feet." In her opinion they looked great, but her feet complained of being pinched and getting blisters. Later when she went back to visit her family in Iowa, she stopped at the local Bauer's shoe store and bought four pairs of shoes from the dollar table to take back with her.

One positive result of the wardrobe change was that the sisters were able to cut up their habits and use the cloth to make their skirts and blouses. Whether the people of Santa Ana thought much about the habit change was hard to tell. Joyce always said, "If they did not want you to know what they were saying, they just sped up their conversation."

School opened in the fall with classes for kindergarten and first grade. Their plan was to add one new grade each year until they had a kindergarten through sixth grade school. They planned to teach English in their school, which typically only happened in wealthy, private schools.

At first they heard a little grumbling from the Assumption sisters because they thought the Madre del Salvador Catholic School might steal some of their students. But it was not a problem because the Assumption school was in a wealthy neighborhood and none of those students would come into the San Raphael barrio. At that time most of the religious orders' schools served primarily the wealthy families of El Salvador. Only the Maryknolls and now the Franciscans served the very poor. Later the Latin American bishops would wonder how the wealthy elite families of El Salvador and other Latin America countries could treat the peasants so poorly after all those years of attending Catholic schools. Some years later many religious orders that had schools in wealthy neighborhoods would start and finance schools in poor areas. In many cases, pass on their old books to them.

It was important progress for San Raphael to get a new Catholic school because many of the government schools were extremely overcrowded, and the teachers may or may not have been interested in teaching. The government schools were sometimes more of a daycare center than an actual school. Many children did not go to school for more than a year or two. Usually it was a long walk and there was always the temptation of going to work and helping to support the family instead of getting an education. Boys were more likely to go to school because the girls could help in the homes. Boys usually would quit when they got old enough to help in the fields. Still today many of the children only make it through sixth grade. Joyce taught first grade with Rosa, her local co-teacher. They called this team style of teaching 'departmental teaching.' In 1963 it was rare, but it has become common in recent years. It made sense to have a local person teach social studies and other courses that required local knowledge.

Madre del Salvador Catholic School was built on a dump and had trains running right through the yard. It had no books - just notebooks, pens, and pencils. Nothing was store-bought; every desk, chair, and school supply used was hand made by the local peasants, students, or the teachers. Yet the school was an overwhelming success. Joyce and Rosa had about twenty to twenty-five students in each of their sections of first grade. Classes started at 8:00 am and lasted until 3:00 pm. Joyce commented that it was a miracle that these small children could come out of poor homes with dirt floors and arrive at school so happy, clean, and alive in their bright uniforms. The sisters bought school uniform material in San Salvador. The boys wore white shirts with gray slacks and the girls wore white blouses with red and white checkered skirts. The students of Madre del Salvador Catholic School were recognized in all of Santa Ana. The teachers taught in the same style, and with the same expectations, as they had when they taught in the United States.

The school had no air conditioning, so it got very hot in the classroom. There was no glass on the windows and with any luck at all, a breeze would blow through the classroom. There was no time for the typical mid-day siesta that most people enjoyed. Joyce remembers dozing off a few times after lunch when the students got into small groups and practiced their reading.

School took a break for Holy Week, and the people loved to form a procession through town with their saint statues to the church. Joyce was often invited to birthday parties with piñatas and great fun was had. There were lots of children and therefore lots of baptisms. Many times the children being baptized were around two or three years old. The same day as the baptism, they would go to the cathedral in the afternoon to be confirmed. The people loved celebrations and First Communion was a favorite. Forty or fifty children, with the girls all dressed up in their very best white dresses and the boys with white shirts and dark slacks made for a beautiful celebration. The people, though desperately poor, had a way to celebrate life.

The Franciscan Sisters at Madre del Salvador School soon discovered that there were hundreds of unemployed teachers in the city of Santa Ana, and the sisters were taking teaching jobs that the local people could use. So within a few years of the start of the school, the North American sisters focused on administration and formation of the local teachers. This change was quite timely because, about at this same time Bishop Graziano came calling, looking for a sister to help fulfill his dream; a school to teach and train rural catechists in a place called El Castaño, in the Diocese of San Miguel.

CHAPTER 3

El Castaño

Today

The Chaparrastique Volcano made for spectacular photos as we traveled along the southwest lowlands. It was among the more active volcanoes in El Salvador and had erupted just a few days ago. On this day, low riding clouds passed by the top of the volcano. Even so, we could still make out a thin trail of smoke ascending from its peak. The road we were traveling on went through a valley just west of the volcano. The countryside was mostly open cattle country with a few sugar cane fields mixed in. Later in the week a Salvadoran would tell us that between the volcanoes, earthquakes and politics, El Salvador was an explosive country.

We were on a mission to find a place called El Castaño, our search having begun in the small village of El Cuco. We had thought El Castaño was on the road we were driving down, but we did not see it. The first few people we asked had never heard of it. Finally, we asked a bus driver and discovered that it was indeed up the road we had just come on, so we started heading back. As we got close to where we thought it should be, we stopped and asked again. Yes, it was just up the road a little farther, and sure enough, there it was behind an old locked gate and a little sign covered with trees and brush that said, "El Castaño."

This was a place very close to Joyce's heart, the place where she had met her good friend, Ann, and for five years experienced the joy of working with small peasant farmers. At El Castaño Sister Joyce would also know betrayal. As we wandered up the trail toward the buildings, Joyce began to remember the El Castaño of almost forty years ago—when grounds were spotless, the buildings were clean and in good repair, and people were working everywhere. El Castaño was alive with activity. Today large leaves covered everything. The building looked unused; it was difficult to believe the lone caretaker when he said they still had meetings here.

The memories came flooding back to Joyce as she explored the building, "Look, here is our old cafeteria, and this was Ann's room, and look, this is where I slept." The facility was located in a beautiful, wooded area overlooking a valley. It would have made a great park. El Castaño is Spanish for 'the chestnut,' and there was one huge chestnut tree still standing. Joyce remembered their being many more. There was also another great climbing tree with outspread, low-hanging limbs, and the youngest member of our group could not resist testing his climbing skills. It was a melancholy trip down memory lane, but as you might expect, it ended with Joyce getting us all invited in to meet the caretaker's family.

It was not difficult imaging a much younger Sister Joyce coming up the lane forty years ago with a hospitable smile, greeting her students—young, shy, peasant farmers who had no clue what they were getting themselves into. Many years later some claim El Castaño and other "training centers" were the catalysts needed to turn poor peasant farmers into activists and eventually revolutionaries.[1] Later, while doing research, we were amazed at the amount of literature that referenced El Castaño and the role it played in the years leading up to the civil war. And here we were, exploring the place with the woman who co-founded the school. El Salvador played a big part in the story of Joyce's life, and it seems, she, at least, played some role in the history of El Salvador.

1965-1971

Bishop Lorenzo Graziano was on a mission. The Maryknoll missionaries had been working for years with the peasants of Guatemala, teaching them how to lead in their small rural churches and communities. In 1968 the Conference of Latin America Bishops resulted in the Medellin Document.[2] In essence, the leadership of the Latin American Church looked at their societies and found them to be very un-Christian. They looked at the partners in power—the generals, the landowners, the elite ruling class and the Church—and had to admit that many deeply rooted values were very unjust. Despite generations of Catholic school education, the values by which they lived, along with the social and economic structures that kept them in power were repressive, corrupt, and even murderous. Named after the city in Columbia where the conference was held, the Medellin Document was the bishops' attempt to apply the teachings of Vatican II to Latin America. It addressed the unjust structures of society, called for land reform and transformation of political structures, and for the Church to reach out to the poor and oppressed rural people. Many priests moved out of their comfortable homes in the cities and went into the countryside to live, work, and give hope to the peasants for the possibility of change.

Bishop Graziano was described as a common man of the people; some would compare him to the current Pope Francis. He often would invite people who had nowhere else to stay into his home. Joyce called him a holy man. The bishop wanted to create a school that would teach the next generation of rural peasants to be catechists of the Church, men who would not only be leaders in their local churches, but in their communities as well.

The Catholic Church in Central America had an extreme shortage of priests. A typical parish might have one priest with thirty thousand parishioners. It was common for a parish to have one primary church in a larger community, and fifteen to forty small chapels in the surrounding villages. These villages were called cantones. In some places the pastor may only visit these cantones once a year to celebrate Mass. Vatican II encouraged lay people to become more involved in the Church's liturgies. If these small chapels were going to have a service every Sunday, the lay people would have to be trained to do it. This is still common today, and many of the small cantones are very organized. Many ministers have had two years of training before they lead a Celebration of the Word service.

The bishop naturally thought of the sisters who were already in the business of education. He reached out to Joyce's community of Franciscans as well as the Dominican Sisters out of Akron, Ohio, who were working in La Union,

El Salvador. The bishop said it was going to be a "mixed marriage" between two orders, which at that time was rarely done. The various orders of sisters tended to be rather competitive and did not want to take the chance that another order would steal away one of their sisters. Joyce did not let such small worries get in her way. She simply went forward and made it work. When Bishop Graziano came to ask Joyce's community who they could send, they looked to the one who was always up for something new. And since they were recruiting local teachers at her current school, Joyce humbly explained "I was the least important at the moment." When she walked into El Castaño that first day she was joined by her soon-to-be dearest friend, Sister Ann Schaefer.

The bishop explained that he wanted his rural priests to recruit local church leaders and bring them to El Castaño for four-week training sessions. Joyce said the Dominicans were the "thinkers and planners," while the Franciscans "made things happen." Ann, who was of the Dominican order, said, "First we must train the priests so they will know what their parishioners are getting into." That's exactly what Joyce put into action. This working arrangement, in which Ann thought and planned things out, and Joyce made those plans a reality, continued for their five years together at El Castaño.

None of the students had cars, so the priests would drive them in on Sunday afternoons and come and pick them up again on Fridays. They went home on weekends to visit their families and to work. During the rainy season many of the thatched roofs would collapse after a week's worth of rain, so many weekends when they went home the men had to replace the roofs. Some men would come back after their four-week training and take another few weeks of classes.

Many of the peasant students had never been to a modern facility like El Castaño. The buildings were relatively new with such modern conveniences as a bathroom with a shower for every two rooms. The United States and Salvadoran governments had built the structures for housing when they were building the Pan America Highway. Bishop Graziano bought the eleven acre complex for $1 from the government. Ann and Joyce had their own rooms and shared a bathroom. The men slept four to a room with two sets of bunk beds and eight men sharing a bathroom. Considering none of these men had used indoor plumbing before this was as good as it gets. Joyce would go check the bathrooms every day to make sure the showers were turned off. Often they were left on because the men had never used a shower before.

The small villages these men lived in were extremely poor. Most homes had dirt floors with no running water or electricity. The people were farmers who grew corn and beans, and maybe raised a few chickens for the eggs. On a special occasion they might kill one of their chickens for dinner, but generally eating meat was rare. They grew most of what they ate, saved some seeds for the next planting, and if they were lucky, they had a little extra to sell. If they worked in coffee, cotton, or sugar cane fields of a large landowner, they could not survive on the wages. Many days the whole family would go out into the fields to work. In the higher altitudes, coffee was the primary crop. Schools would be closed November through January during the coffee harvest so the kids could join their parents picking coffee. They were paid so much per bucket of coffee picked so everyone could help the family survive. Every day the women would make corn tortillas by hand. First they would grind the corn, mix it with water to make a flour paste, shape the tortillas, and then cook them on a primitive flat-topped stove fueled with wood. It was time-consuming, difficult labor, but corn tortillas are a staple in Central American diets, eaten for breakfast, lunch, and dinner. Another household chore was laundry, which was usually taken and washed in the closest stream. It was a tough life and any problems with a crop or employer could lead to hunger.

On the men's first day, Joyce met them as they walked up the lane to El Castaño. Their first sight was the grand chestnut trees and immaculate grounds, followed by the fantastic facilities, and of course, this larger-than-life smiling woman, Sister Joyce. Though she no longer wore a habit, there was no mistaking that she was a religious sister.

The students may have been peasants, but they were smart and already leaders in their communities. However, this experience was something completely foreign to them. Most had never traveled this far from home and likely had never ridden in a car or truck. The fact that their priest had invited them out of all the people from their villages was a huge honor and very exciting. They had no idea what to expect and, understandably, were feeling nervous, timid, and a bit overwhelmed when they walked up the lane. Joyce, on the other hand, happily greeted many groups of new students. She claims she too was feeling a little shy and timid, but if you know Sister Joyce, you would find this is hard to believe. Even if she was, it's likely the men never noticed as she welcomed them with a hug and probably said something like, "Welcome! Look who the Spirit has brought to our school."

Anthropologist Leigh Binford interviewed El Castaño graduates for a study called "Peasants, Catechists, and Revolutionaries." Student Miguel Angel Benitez commented for the study 'What are we going to do here? I had thought they were (only) going to teach us about the bible and prayer...."[3]

They did pray and study scripture, but that was only one class of many. Ann wrote the curriculum and had almost every minute of the day planned. A typical day would start at sunrise or earlier with a simple meal of corn tortillas and oatmeal. The first class of the day was taught by one of several priests including Father Dennis St. Marie from the Diocese of Cleveland. Father Dennis was the director of El Castaño and also the pastor of a local parish. He did not live at El

Castaño but commuted to teach and say Mass. If the priests for whatever reason could not make it to class, Ann or Joyce substituted. During the cooler times of day the students would sit at round tables outside under the chestnut trees rather than in their classrooms.

The purpose of the religion class was to train the men to lead Liturgy of the Word celebrations and to be Eucharistic Ministers. Since most of the men couldn't read, Joyce designed bible story charts with symbols and pictures instead of words. She invited a Sister with artistic skills to paint it onto the canvas cloth, which was eight feet long by three feet tall, waterproof and very durable. The men could roll up the charts and take them to teach in their home communities. If the men came back for further training, they would get the next chart in the series.

One of the primary ideas taught using these charts was salvation history. The history of salvation starts with creation, explores the prophets of the Old Testament, then the New Testament, and concludes with the teachings of the Church. The Creation Story was the first of many instances where these peasant leaders, or catechists as they were called at El Castaño, would begin to learn that God loved all people equally, and it was not God's will for them to be poor or to suffer. They learned that God had created the world and all of its resources for everyone, not only for the elite. When Joyce taught the story of Moses and the liberation of the Israeli people from the Egyptians, the men recognized that they too were an oppressed people.

The men also received their own New Testament bibles. Joyce loved to watch her students' eyes light up and hear them say, "Wait until I get home and show my wife!" As the men gradually improved their reading skills, they loved to study the New Testament. They often heard ministers from other religions quoting bible verses. Sometimes they pointed out to Joyce that the verses they were quoting did not say what these ministers had claimed. Joyce only hoped her students would take what they learned at El Castaño and share it with their neighbors back in their cantones.

Daily religion class was followed by some kind of agricultural training, working in the fields planted on the grounds while it was still relatively cool outside. By the end of the agriculture class, it was time for a simple lunch of beans, rice, and corn tortillas, followed by a siesta. Ann ran a tight ship, but it did include time for a nap, which of course, made good sense because there was no air conditioning, and it was hot.

Following the siesta was usually another agriculture class and then a public health class. As community leaders, they often dealt with health issues. Not only did the men learn about personal hygiene, they also learned useful things that could be put into practice in their villages. The last class before dinner was basic reading, writing, and math. Very few of the men knew how to read before coming to El Castaño, and Joyce loved to see them using the New Testament bibles while they sounded out the words. To finish the day, there was a simple meal and maybe some kind of presentation before everyone went to bed at sundown. Throughout the whole day Joyce was kept busy sitting in on classes and making sure everything was running just the way Ann planned it.

Joyce said her students learned deep respect, the beauty of themselves, and that we all share in the same humanity. She taught them that they too are important, loved, and with rights and responsibilities. The process they followed at El Castaño led to a new empowerment—an awareness of their freedom and of being children of God. With this new understanding, they would begin to think critically and take action to solve their problems. If the men came back for a second or third round of classes their education was centered on their individual gifts and work in their communities: Ministers of the Word, Eucharistic ministers, public health, reading teachers, etc. By the Sisters' second year at El Castaño, they had created a real Universidad Campesina—a school specifically for educating the local farmers.

Sister Ann grew up in Johnstown, Pennsylvania as Elizabeth Ann Schaefer. She was known officially in the Catholic Church as Sister Mary Bonaventure,

but when she went to El Salvador, she changed her name back to Ann because it was easier for the people to say. Ann and two other Dominican Sisters were part of the Cleveland Latin America Mission team, from the Diocese of Cleveland. They were working in La Union when Bishop Graziano recruited Ann to come to El Castaño. Joyce and Ann had gone to training together in Guatemala and other places. When they joined forces at El Castaño they already knew each other, but neither the Bishop nor anyone else could have known what a great team and friendship they would form.

Joyce was the farm girl—active, very hard working, organized, and handy with a lot of farm girl common sense. Ann grew up in the city, was smart, educated, and knew how to plan and solve problems. Ann and Joyce loved their vows and the outdoors. Every day they would pray the Divine Praises outside in the kiosco (a gazebo).

The Sisters kept a rule at El Castaño: once a week they would get away just to help each other keep their sanity. One thing they both had in common was that they knew how to have fun. Usually Joyce and Ann would head to the beach, which was just a short twenty minute drive. Once in a while the sisters from Santa Ana would join them for the day. The area was rural, so they mostly had the beach to themselves for an afternoon of swimming, sunbathing, and a picnic lunch. On one trip they were joined by one of the sisters from Santa Ana and her father who was visiting from the United States. On the way home, the van they were driving overheated, a common issue in that hot climate. The Sister's father asked if they had any coke left, which they did; so they replaced the water lost from the radiator with Coke and off they went with no further problems.

At the end of the fourth week of classes the staff took a break for a few weeks. The priests needed time in their parishes, so Joyce and Ann hit the road and visited their graduates. They traveled all over southern El Salvador. Sometimes it was a six hour drive or more to get where they were going. There were no rest stops, and a call from nature meant a hike into the woods. The civil war had not yet begun, and if violence was occurring in the countryside, Ann and Joyce were not aware of it. They calmly traveled in the most isolated places with no worries at all.

The roads to the rural cantones were terrible enough in the dry season, but in the rainy season they were even worse. Ann drove their 4-wheel drive Jeep when she had to, but it was not one of her favorite things to do. They often had to drive through flooded roads, which terrified Ann. She seemed to have this natural ability to find every big rock hidden in the water. Joyce, on the other hand, loved driving, and as an old farm girl was quite good at avoiding the rocks and ruts in the road. Driving, fixing things, and a love of simple people were in Joyce's rural genes. They would often listen to Bishop Oscar Romero on the radio. Ann played a trumpet and she loved to play it out of the Jeep window, announcing their arrival as they drove into cantones. The villagers would come running at the sound. The people loved Joyce and Ann as much as the sisters loved the rural Salvadorans. They would spend a day or two in the cantones working with their former students. They would sleep in any house that offered to take them in, but usually their nights were spent sleeping on the chapel pews. What a joy it was for Joyce and Ann to just live the Gospel with these humble, rural families who were really not that different from the Iowans that Joyce grew up with.

The Medellin Document stated: "The Church—the People of God—will lend its support to the downtrodden of every social class so that they might come to know their rights and how to make use of them."[2] That statement describes exactly what Joyce and Ann were trying to do at El Castaño. While the term "liberation theology" was not used until 1971, the ideas for it were already being developed by the priests and sisters working with the poor in Central and South America.

Liberation theology can be described as faith that emphasizes the needs of the poor and encourages them "to read the Scripture in a way that affirms their dignity and self-worth and their right to struggle together for a more decent life."[4] It is an understanding of theology in which God wants His people to work toward building the kingdom of heaven in our world here and now.

El Salvador was a place that desperately needed liberation. The United States government has a long history in El Salvador. In 1931 Major AJ Harris of the United States military attaché warned that the country was ripe for revolution. He said of El Salvador "I learned that roughly 90% of the wealth of the nation is held by about .05% of the population. Thirty or forty families own nearly everything in the country. They live in almost regal style ... The rest of the population has practically nothing."[5] In 1932 the Salvadoran poor did revolt, but it was brutally put down by the military when they slaughtered between 20,000 to 30,000 people.[6] When the government stopped the killing, the peasants quietly returned to their former place in society, and it was much the same when Joyce arrived in El Salvador in 1963. In the 1970's, when it once again appeared revolution was likely to happen, the elite of El Salvador speculated on how many peasants they would have to kill this time to keep them in their place.

The United States had long supported the government of El Salvador supposedly because of the fear of communism. Ironically, the Vatican was soon to join the United States in supporting the status quo. Although the Latin American Bishops believed the people had a right to try to improve their lives, Pope John Paul II reacted strongly against liberation theology. The Pope was a staunch opponent of communism, and did everything in his power to end liberation theology. His primary tactic was to appoint conservative bishops in Latin America who supported his views.

In 1984 Pope John Paul II visited Nicaragua to voice his opposition to the Sandinista revolutionary leaders, who were supported by the local Catholic Church. Three times over the course of his speech the Pope had to yell "Silence!" at the crowd as they heckled him. Some observers interpreted this as symbolic of his "silencing" of the theology and those that supported it.[7] Joyce knew that many United States and some Latin American bishops and priests did not support liberation theology, but she also knew none of them personally lived and worked with the poor of Central America, and therefore could not understand. The theology was so simple to Joyce; she said "It says all people were equal in God's eyes, and had a right to try and improve their lives, however if the poor improved their lives then it would mean the wealthy would also have to change, and this was not a part of their plans."

The priests and sisters working in El Salvador were putting the teachings of Vatican II and the Medellin Document into practice. At El Castaño the students' eyes were opened as they began to realize they had dignity in the sight of God. By the time they went home after four weeks of classes, they believed they had a right to try and improve their lives. Later people said El Castaño and other schools like it were the catalysts that transformed their peasant students into activists and ultimately into revolutionaries.[1] Many of the students did indeed try to organize the people of their communities.

For example, one group of former students created a savings and loan cooperative to provide low interest loans to the local farmers.[3] This type of enterprise helped free the people from the economic oppression by the elite landowners. Thus the landowners saw this as a threat to be eliminated at all costs. Ironically, the bishop bought the school from the government and the government provided and paid the lay teachers. But that did not mean the government was not keeping tabs on what was happening. At this time the military had not yet started to target and murder members of religious communities. Even so, the team at El Castaño progressed with caution. For example, they called their students 'catechists' instead of 'leaders.' The Maryknolls had used the term 'leaders' in Guatemala and the military had aggressively persecuted them for it. Joyce only knew she had a deep love for the people and her God; she and Ann were simple people just trying to live the gospel as they had been called.

By their fifth year at El Castaño the political situation in the country had grown much worse. In Guatemala civil war had erupted and had already been raging for several years. The military there was murdering people in the countryside by the thousands. Even though the murders had not started yet in El Salvador, Joyce and Ann were constantly aware of the possibility and kept a close eye on their students. They began to notice some subtle changes in behavior from the government-funded agricultural teacher. Joyce could not put her finger on it at the time, but she started to suspect that he was reporting back to the government about the activities at El Castaño. Joyce and Ann discussed what they should do about it and finally Joyce decided to talk to the director of El Castaño, Father Dennis St. Marie. At the staff meeting Father, Ann and Joyce were sitting outside in the shade on a hot day. When Joyce told Father what she suspected was going on, he reacted with anger. Within minutes he asked her to leave El Castaño and essentially fired her on the spot. To Father's great surprise Ann spoke up and said, "Then we go together." Just like that their work at El Castaño was finished, and they were gone in less than twenty-four hours.

Why did Father react so strongly? Joyce was never sure because they didn't get the chance to ask him. Father did not live at El Castaño but only came in to teach and say Mass. In effect he just did what Ann told him to do, and so he probably had not been aware of the things that Joyce and Ann saw every day. It was hot, and tempers could run short in the tropics. Maybe it was as simple as that, and once he let Joyce go and Ann joined her, there was no way to take it back.

Joyce's response was perhaps one of a little relief, hurt, and finally just shaking the dust off her feet in a place that no longer welcomed her. It must have been time to move on. Later Joyce would say that this was not the only time she parted ways with an employer in a less than agreeable way, and each time it has caused her pain. But she has a joy and spirit about her that just cannot be held down. Later Sister would journal:

Parting Ways

"What a blessing.... You have given us so much, we now return it to You. Yes, I have been fired a few times on my journey of faith. Thank You God for a support team, a spiritual director, etc. to always keep me walking. "You're fired...I want you to leave in two weeks." These are harsh words, yet I have learned much from receiving these loud commands and I have always walked away with so much peace. Praise God for those friends, teams, and pilgrims who saw good in me. How well I could take up the cross without being crucified. Yes, how blessed I have been to walk with empowered people... I have refused to be destroyed for I have been called and recognized the power in me."

Joyce was shocked and overjoyed that Ann walked out in solidarity with her. Unlike Joyce, Ann was leaving her own Cleveland Diocesan Mission team. To this day Joyce speaks of her great love and admiration for Ann. Ann returned to the United States shortly after she left El Castaño and went on to a very successful career in education and leadership for her order. She and Ann had created something special at El Castaño; together they touched many lives.

CHAPTER 4

Veintidós de Abril

Today

The mother and her daughter were there purely by chance. They were in the wrong place at the wrong time. For that matter, the Jesuit priests had moved to these quarters because they thought it would be safer than their regular rooms. They were wrong. When the military surrounded the campus with three hundred and fifty troops there was no chance of escape.

We were visiting the housing unit where the Salvadoran military, supported by the United States government, murdered Julia Elba Ramos, her daughter Celina, and six Jesuit priests: Ignacio Ellacuria, Juan Ramon Moreno, Joaquin Lopez y Lopez, Ignacio Martin Baro, Amando Lopez, and Segundo Montes. With the exception of Sister Joyce, no one in our group had witnessed this kind of violence.

Visiting the Monsignor Romero Center and the Martyr's Memorial Room was not a pleasant experience. The clothing the victims wore the day they were murdered was on display. Even more difficult to view were the graphic photos taken of the bodies immediately after the murders. These photos were located in albums locked away in a small room. We did not have to view them, but for some reason it seemed important. It is hard to imagine how anyone could resort to this kind of violence to maintain power, and it's even harder to understand how the United States government could support it. Earlier in the week we had visited the shrine and the place where the murdered bodies had been found of the lay minister, Jean Donovan and three Maryknoll Sisters: Ita Ford, M.M, Maura Clark, M.M, Carla Piette, M.M. These four women were kidnapped, raped, and murdered in 1980. The six Jesuits and the mother and daughter were killed in 1989.

We were exploring in many ways a difficult time in Sister's ministry in El Salvador and a tragic time in the life of the country. The civil war lasted from 1979 to 1992, and the United Nations estimates over 75,000 people were killed.

But the violence, as Joyce can testify to, started much earlier. She had served the peasants who were migrating to the city of San Salvador looking for work and to escape the violence in the countryside. Unfortunately, the violence followed them to the city.

      This is the story of Veintidós de Abril. We were searching for a community center that Joyce had helped build in the neighborhood. We hired a driver because we needed someone familiar with the city and surrounding country. As we slowly drove up the street, it looked just like many other villages in El Salvador. The streets were crowded and busy with street vendors and shops. The only real difference was the extensive graffiti on pretty much every exposed wall space. Our driver, Leo, seemed to be a little anxious. Finally, he said we needed to turn around and get out of Veintidós de Abril. Apparently the people were still living with violence, only this time the violence was gang-related. Leo pointed out the gang symbols in the graffiti and decided it was not safe for us to stay in Veintidós de Abril.

1971-1974

One outcome from the severe shortage of priests was the concept of Christian Base Communities. Because of her work at El Castaño and her six months of studying in Ecuador, Joyce was at the forefront of this movement. These communities were usually made up of ten to twenty families and could be located in either rural or urban areas. Their goals included developing catechists and leadership for the local churches while also allowing the people to work together to improve their own lives. Of course any activity that worked to free the poor from the unjust economic structures in El Salvador was viewed as a threat to the ruling class and was opposed by whatever means necessary. More and more those means included kidnapping, torturing, and murdering those who organized and led these kinds of groups.

After Joyce left El Castaño, she spent a short time with her sisters in Santa Ana but soon moved to a small apartment near Saint Francis Church in the center of San Salvador. The pastor was Monsignor Urioste. Joyce had met him several times over the past few years, but now they really came to know each other. Urioste was well known in El Salvador, and would eventually become a good friend of Bishop Oscar Romero. Later he would often travel around the world to attend meetings and conferences at the requests of the Salvadoran bishops. For the moment he would send young sisters to accompany the tall North American sister who was working so closely with the people. For the next few years this became a regular practice. Monsignor and religious communities would send their new members in El Salvador to Joyce to learn what being a missionary was all about. The trust they put in Joyce was really quite astounding when you recognize how carefully each order resisted allowing its sisters to mingle with those of another order.

The next year was a busy time for Joyce. While at El Castaño she had been appointed to the Board of Directors of the religious organization CONFER, which represented all the priests, sisters, and brothers in El Salvador; it was similar to a business trade group. In addition to attending local meetings, she traveled to Peru to represent the group at a conference. During this time she also spent a semester at the bishops' Pastoral Institute of Latin America in Quito, Ecuador. Among a variety of other courses Joyce studied liberation theology, Christian Base Communities, and anthropology. She enjoyed a week participating in anthropological studies in a rural indigenous village where she observed that the native people had "the most lovely pink cheeks."

The Pastoral Institute was part of the bishop's effort to apply the teachings that came out of Vatican II and the Medellin Document. Joyce was not just on the cutting edge of the movement—she really worked in the trenches with these new concepts. She could share the realities of the Church's new methods on reaching out to the poor. Father Jose Marins, who taught at the Institute and would later recruit Joyce to join his team of leadership trainers, wrote that the Latin America Bishops considered Christian Base Communities to be an important pastoral option. He taught that the Church served the world and the base community was the most basic level of the Church.

Try to imagine a diagram where you start with the base community and surround it with the parish, then the diocese, then the universal Church, and finally the world around it all. The most important level is the base community where the people of the Church live. All other levels ought to be in service to this basic level and not the other way around.[1] Service was what Joyce did—her whole being lived to serve the poor people she loved. Imagine a world where government and church leaders followed this model.

Joyce soon moved on to work in the parish of Santa Lucia, which was located in a poor barrio on the outskirts of San Salvador. Her friend Ann and another Sister had started a ministry there but now were returning to the United States, so Joyce moved in to continue their work. Initially she lived with a barber and his family. Families would start with a single room shack and over the years add on and make improvements. They built a little room for Joyce behind their house and the whole family shared their one bathroom with her. She now wore a simple dress with a cross hanging around her neck. She washed her clothes by hand in a small pila, or sink, and hung them out to dry.

While she lived with the barber's family, her parents came to El Salvador to visit. It was her parents' first time flying in an airplane, and Joyce thought it a small miracle that they flew all the way from Omaha, Nebraska, to San Salvador by themselves. They visited the convent in Santa Ana and even spent one night in Joyce's small room. She had a couple of what they called "scissor beds" that folded out. Joyce's parents loved her, and her father was especially proud of his 'Sister Joyce.' They spent several weeks with Joyce and travelled all over the country with her, except back to the El Castaño area where she did not feel welcome. On their last night in El Salvador they stayed at a rather run down convent near the airport. Unfortunately the mosquitoes were terrible, and they left town itchy and tired, but overall it was a great trip, and they were able to see Joyce's role in the community and the love the Salvadorans had for her.

Santa Lucia was a large parish that included several barrio neighborhoods. Each neighborhood had a name based on a date. For example, one was called Primero de Mayo, or May 1st. Joyce's time was spent visiting the families in the parish. She would walk down the dirt roads, or on the railroad tracks which once again ran right through the community. Children were everywhere as she went about ministering to the people and organizing Christian Base Communities.

Santa Lucia had a strong team with planning meetings every week. They were busy with Bible groups at night, liturgies on the weekend, baptisms, funerals, and all of the activities that make up a large parish. And of course, they had their fair share of tragedies.

One morning around nine, Joyce heard screaming nearby. As she ran over, she could see families huddled around a small boy who had been crushed by a truck. Joyce joined the family as they all sat on the curb of the road saying "Hail Mary's" together. They had a wake for the child throughout the night and in the morning had a funeral and a procession to the cemetery. For the next nine days they held prayer vigils in the family's home. This would be repeated every year on the anniversary of his death.

The city, and especially the poor areas around Santa Lucia, was growing rapidly. The peasant farmers were being forced off their land, and there were no jobs in the countryside. Tensions were rising between the farmers and Catholic Religious on one side, and the wealthy elite landowners and the government on the other. People were moving to the city in hopes of finding jobs and safety. Some foreign companies were beginning to relocate to Central America to reduce their costs for labor. In the Santa Lucia area a large calculator manufacturing plant had opened. The pay was terrible, the working conditions difficult, but the people were desperate for jobs. U.S. corporations' practice of relocating manufacturing facilities to countries with no or little labor protection is another example of how the U.S. takes advantage of poor people to keep prices low and profits high.

The vast majority of these new families were settling in places like the area Santa Lucia served, which were on the outskirts of the city and usually on very steep hills. Because the only fuel for cook stoves was wood, these hills were quickly becoming deforested. During the rainy season Joyce was called to a mudslide in an area consisting of about eighty shacks. One shack was almost completely covered. She found herself digging with other families and friends using whatever tools they could find, but mostly with just their bare hands. With great joy they pulled out an old grandmother and a small child, both terrified but alive and well. The image is still vividly planted in her memory.

Once a month Joyce would travel across town to attend the CONFER meetings. By this time she had become president of the group. She also travelled to Santa Ana to meet with and have some fun with her fellow sisters. On a few occasions they would be joined by any other English speaking people that happened to be in the area: Peace Corp members, Mormon boys on mission, or sisters from other orders. It didn't matter who, just the fact that they were all in El Salvador and spoke English gave them enough in common to have a good time together.

Walking the dirt streets of the barrio was always eventful. Stray dogs were everywhere, but there was not a cat to be found. The dogs were skinny, many sickly-looking. They ran in packs and sometimes were aggressive. In the rainy season it was nice to be carrying an umbrella to fight off the stray dog, or two, if you had to.

Joyce and the parish team often met to discuss how to deal with social issues. It was always hot, and with so many people out of work, alcohol was a problem which led to domestic abuse and fights on the street. They parish team worked on things as simple as dealing with the terrible fly problem to things as complex as job creation and holding their ground against the government.

Joyce had first-hand experience with the scourge of alcohol. The barber she was living with had a part-time job in a pharmacy and began to drink some kind of alcohol he was getting from work. He never did abuse Joyce or the family as far as she knew, but eventually it got so bad, she felt compelled to move out. She moved into a house owned by a carpenter with two other sisters. His wife and two teenagers also lived in the home. It was a slightly older neighborhood, so the house was little a more established.

The sisters had a hot plate in their room, but it would take hours to make beans. The carpenter's wife, on the other hand, made beans in a big pot out on the patio over a wood fire. They were fantastic, and the sisters soon added their beans to her pot. Their room had two sets of bunk beds, and their clothes would hang from the ceiling. The sisters prayed in community. Every day the youngest Sister would go to school to learn to read while Joyce and Sister Lucinda would walk down the tracks to visit families in the parish.

The influx of people had created a serious shortage of housing. While the government was opening some new housing developments, it fell far short of the need. The people grew tired of getting few results out of the government's promises for more housing. On April 22nd a mob of about one thousand people occupied a city dump. The people arrived with a few pieces of clothing, some plastic, and a stick to prop up the plastic for cover. The city mayor, who had been promising housing for years, showed up at 5:30 in the morning saw all the people, shook his head, and said: "Stay put, I will see what we can do." The people never

did leave, and thus the community of Veintedós Abril (22nd of April) was born. Joyce and the people of Santa Lucia built a community building in the heart of Veintedós Abril, and it became a very busy social hub for the area. Joyce spent many hours there working on one project or another.

The government and the military began to step up their counter-insurgency activities. As early as 1963, the United States government sent military advisors to El Salvador to help train and organize these efforts. The Nationalist Democratic Organization, (ORDEN) was created specifically to carry out counter-insurgency actions. ORDEN had brigades in every hamlet and village; it carried out a regular patrolling system, including all-night road blocks, and actively collected intelligence on subversion.[2] The group may have started with the goal of collecting intelligence but it soon crossed the line to violence. In the later 60's, 70's, and throughout the civil war death squads with names like the "White Hands" branched off from ORDEN and other paramilitary groups.[3] These death squads were responsible for thousands of the "disappeared."

The locals used the term los desaparecidos, or "the disappeared," to refer to the victims because that was exactly what happened: they would just go missing in the night. Sometimes they would be released alive after being tortured, or after a few days their body would be found. The violence reached its peak during the civil war. Religious orders were specifically targeted, which resulted in dozens of murdered priests and sisters. It was especially dangerous for Jesuits because the military believed they were advocating and supporting revolution. Joyce worked with several priests who were later murdered.

One priest she worked with and had a deep respect for was the Jesuit, Rutilio Grande, a parish priest and outspoken advocate for the poor. He, an old man, and a sixteen year boy were machine-gunned down as they were driving to a village Mass. At one point the death squads were so visible in the country that the people became aware they had created the slogan, "Kill a priest a day." There were so many people disappearing that a mothers group formed called the "Committee of the Mothers of the Disappeared and Assassinated of El Salvador," or Co-Madres. Bishop Oscar Romero encouraged them to organize. Their main work was to document and protest the cases of the disappeared. They would march in the streets wearing black dresses and white headbands holding up pictures of the disappeared.[4] Salvadorans have a history of resistance and protesting injustice.

While Joyce was working in Santa Lucia, protesters occupied the San Salvador Cathedral. Police and military surrounded the church and would only let priests and sisters come and go. For two or three days Joyce and her fellow sisters would bring in water and food to the protestors. Joyce, by virtue of being the president of CONFER, was asked to speak to the group. At one point in her talk she told the crowd "We support their efforts." Later in the day a fellow Sister asked her what she meant by saying we support them. The military was right outside and could possibly hear her talking. In any case there were informers mixed in with every crowd and it was a very dangerous comment. Fortunately this protest was in the early years before the government would risk kidnapping foreign religious.

Sadly, through all the violence the United States government was providing military support to the Salvadoran government. Only when on December 2, 1980, the North American lay woman Jean Donovan and the three U.S. sisters Maura Clark M.M., Ita Ford, M.M., and Carla Piette, M.M. were kidnapped, raped, and murdered, did the U.S. public take notice. The Carter administration then put some pressure on the Salvadoran government. The United States suspended aid to El Salvador's military, but it appeared to be more of an attempt to avoid a public relations nightmare, and within a few weeks most of the aid had been resumed.[5] Several years later the investigation into the women's murder resulted in the arrest and conviction of several low-ranking Salvadoran guardsmen. No effort was made to determine who actually ordered the murders, though it was clear to all that these murders had indeed been ordered by higher-ranking officials in the government. The Reagan administration resisted any effort to pursue the guilty party. Jean Kilpatrick, then Ambassador to the United Nations, even went so far as to accuse the women of being political activists for a revolutionary group, saying that was what caused them to be targeted.[5]

During Joyce's time ministering to the people of Santa Lucia, it became more and more common for people to disappear. Women would come to Joyce crying, "My husband or son did not come home from work, please come with me to find him." Joyce recalls one morning when Lucinda came to her crying that her husband did not return from work the day before. "Please help me look for him." she said. Sister and Lucinda followed her husband's route to work. Sister remembers walking the entire way and the horrific sight of finding body parts strewn in the ditch alongside the road. They were only able to identify Lucinda's husband by the shirt he wore. They gathered up some pieces of his body and his shirt, put them in a plastic bag and took them back to Veintidós de Abril for a funeral ceremony. This was a terrible task that Joyce almost numbly performed, but she knew she had to help the family and just be present with them in their anguish and pain. These were dark days that Joyce rarely speaks about, but she did share her thoughts in the following journal entry.

What Is Being Free?

It was a call to risk... loving Christ and letting go of all the rest. With the murdered thousands—priests, sisters, laity... leaders were missing—that was the suffering church.

I love my church and only wanted to live the gospel. These same words were uttered by St. Francis years ago as he knelt in Rome before the Holy Father pleading for the approval of the Franciscan Rule over 100 years ago.

We were living the truth. Often the First World tried to hide the truth. That is what power does. We all know that the killings of six Jesuits made news. The assassination of 75,000 people in El Salvador unfortunately doesn't make news. The more than 30 million people around the world who die yearly due to hunger or diseases related to hunger also make no news.

Poverty is not only lacking opportunity but much more. Maybe 60, 70, 80 per cent of people are only trying to survive daily. People want to organize to take back their lives. Oscar Romero would say that there are two idols, wealth and military. Those who disagree with power get killed by the army. Touch the idol and you will be killed. Missionaries just tell and live the truth. The lies came forth, the same happened to Jesus Christ, to Martin Luther King, Jr. and Romero. What a world we live in. So much death and suffering; where is hope? How can people not commit collective suicide with so many centuries of oppression and repression? Victoria from Guatemala tells us, "Because we have hope, we search for freedom. In my country it was not possible. Nothing was safe for my family. I had to leave."

One evening when Joyce returned home, the carpenter said some military men had stopped at their house and started asking questions about the tall woman who lived with him. The religious had a protocol for when something like this happened. Joyce immediately went to see Archbishop Chavez, Bishop Rivera Damas, Monsignor Urioste, and several others who had formed a team that monitored threats to the religious. This group had heard there was a list of twelve religious that were targeted to disappear; the soldier's appearance at her home convinced them that Joyce's name was on that list. They gave her specific orders: no going out at night, no traveling alone, and she was to report any suspicious activity. Later as Joyce reflected on the threat, she concluded it was probably a result of her work in El Castaño.

Within a few days word came to Joyce that she needed to go to Santa Ana and speak with the sister who handled communication from the motherhouse in La Crosse, Wisconsin. The leadership was ordering her to move. A long discussion ensued in which the two women tried to determine if this meant she must change location and ministries, or just find a new place to live and continue her work in Santa Lucia. Of course we know what Joyce was arguing for and that is why the conversation lasted as long as it did. Finally it was decided she could continue her work in Santa Lucia but she would have to find a new place to live. Through all of this Joyce was never afraid for herself. She loved her God and the Spirit moved her to do His will. Joyce writes about fear.

How Could She Be Afraid?

"What about fear? Fear is so enslaving and so I work to relieve myself of this fear syndrome. Who am I meant to be? This is what I need to strive for at all times."

"Marriages were broken, families divided and Church and government was challenged. I was in no fear. The United States heard the stories on T.V. and the news. This was true gospel living and apostles cannot do mission in fear. I was so in love with my God, and the power of the Holy Spirit was so present in me."

CHAPTER 5

Leadership Training

Today

Of all the people Joyce came to know and love in El Salvador, Monsignor Ricardo Urioste was perhaps the one Joyce worked with most closely over the greatest number of years. Our travels had taken us to the Monsignor Romero Center at the University of Central America in San Salvador. Father Jose, with the help of the local bishop, had arranged for us to visit with Monsignor Urioste. Joyce had worked with him while he was a pastor in San Salvador. Later he became the Vicar General for Archbishop Romero. When we visited with him, near the age of ninety, he was still driving and still the president of the Monsignor Oscar Arnulfo Romero Foundation.

From left to right:

Tim Sullivan, Pat Graeve Michels, Msgr. Ricardo Urioste, Father Jose Reynaldo Hernadez, Charlotte Willenborg and Sister Joyce Blum

Monsignor Urioste graciously shared with us a talk he had given in London about Archbishop Romero. He was a champion for the cause of sainthood for Romero, but what we really hoped for was to hear stories of his time working with Joyce and the Christian Base Communities. On the day we were with him it was clear he had had a long and full life. Joyce had considered him an older priest even when she was working in El Salvador. After a few questions it was evident he no longer remembered much from those days, but the respect Joyce showed him and the love and joy on her face as she spoke with him told us the only story we needed.

Joyce seemed to live out of a suitcase. She was always traveling here or there for training (which she was usually leading), making trips into the countryside, visiting parishes, or quite often looking for new place to live. Once every five years she went home to visit her family. Her mom and dad constantly worried about Joyce's safety. They did not really want Joyce to be in El Salvador in the first place, but of course they supported her decision. Her brother Charley said there was a bounty on Joyce, and he was just waiting for the day when they would call and say they had found Joyce's body beside the road. Charlie knew the stories about how Joyce always took a different way home, and if she was driving alone, she would put a hat in the back window to make it look like someone was riding with her. Joyce had asked her parents' permission to be buried in El Salvador if something did happen to her. Her parents refused and said they would send the Franciscans the money to bring her back.

However, there were fun stories as well. For example, Joyce's mom once gave her a watch, and by the next time she came home, it was gone because Joyce had given it away. That's the way it went from then on—every trip home Joyce got a new watch to replace the one she had given away in El Salvador. Ann Dols from St. Theresa's Catholic Church in Des Moines made the following comment about Joyce,

> "Sister has this wonderful ability to appreciate everything material, yet not be attached to it. She sees beauty in so much of the world, but desires so few material things. If some material thing does come into her possession, it burns a hole in her pocket, until she finds a home for it and gives it away."

And now she was once again looking for a new home. Sometimes it was challenging to find a good place to live. After the threats on her life and the orders to move from her superiors, Joyce decided it would be best if she lived in a convent, or at least with a group of sisters. The Franciscans did not have a convent anywhere close to her work in Santa Lucia, so she went knocking on the doors of other religious orders. At the time, although sisters from different orders might be working together, rarely was a sister allowed to live in the convent of a religious order not her own. Joyce asked one order if they had room, and yes, they had room, but, they did not allow that sort of thing. Joyce knocked on a second religious' order door and got the same reply.

Finally she asked the Assumption sisters if she could stay with them, the response was: "Probably not, but you will have to talk to our Major Superior when she returns." A few days later she met with the Major Superior[6] and asked if she could live with them. She replied, "They had room, but she didn't really think it was such a good idea. It seems they had bent the rules once before and let a few Maryknoll sisters live with them. Those sisters had kept all kinds of strange hours. They never knew when the Maryknolls might come home. Sometimes it wasn't until the middle of the night". Joyce said she would keep regular hours, be home early, and if she was out late it meant she was traveling out to a village to do training with Monsignor Urioste. That was probably what tipped the balance in her favor. Monsignor was well known and well respected.

Joyce wanted to make things simple for the Assumption sisters and their staff, so she said she would join them for daily prayers, but they said, "No, you cannot join us for prayers."

Joyce responded, "OK, I understand, but I will eat with the sisters to save your cook the trouble." But Major Superior again said, "No, you cannot eat with the sisters; our cook would prepare something separate for you." In the end it all worked out and Joyce stayed with the Assumption sisters until she left El Salvador.

Joyce had met Father Jose Marins in Quito, Ecuador, at the bishop's Latin American Institute. Father Marins was a leading theologian on Christian Base Communities and had been the bishop's theologian advisor at the Medellin Conference. He recruited Joyce to join his four person team as they traveled around Central and North America conducting training for the leadership of the Catholic Church. She never gave it a second thought, but this was quite an honor! If you looked up the word humility in the dictionary, Joyce's picture would probably be there.

Father Marins already had two members on his team who he had worked with in the past. Out of all the people who had attended the Institute, he invited Joyce to join them. He may have asked Joyce because she was already putting the ideas into practice in her ministries, or because she had this joyful, larger-than-life personality, or just because she was a lot of fun. Or maybe it was because he could not find anyone else crazy enough to spend a year traveling with such a grueling schedule. In any case, this training was for the top leadership of the church. Bishop Oscar Romero took the training, as did Archbishop Luis Chavez, of San Salvador. This is where Joyce got to know Chavez so well. For close to a year they traveled all over Central America, Mexico, and even had training sessions in San Antonio, Texas, and Phoenix, Arizona. They slept wherever the diocese put them, conducted training Monday through Friday, and then moved

---

[6]The Assumption Major Superior was responsible for all the Assumption sisters in Central America.

on to the next stop over the weekend. Bishops, heads of seminaries, superiors of religious communities, and the top 40 to 60 Catholic leaders in whatever area they happened to be in attended the workshops.

They would start with the Old Testament, work through the Prophets, the New Testament, Vatican II, and the Medellin Document, and tie it all to Christian Base Communities. The term "liberation theology" was coined by Father Gustavo Gutierrez about the same year this training was taking place, and you can be sure the theology was thoroughly examined. The workshops included lots of discussion. You can just imagine the excitement of sitting around a table discussing these very new theologies and their relevance to the ministries of the church leaders in Latin America.

One of the core ideas was that God created us as one human family and loved each of us good or bad, rich or poor, equally. God does not intend for us to suffer. On the contrary, he wants us to live our lives to the fullest. Since God created us equals and Jesus taught not to use titles, everyone was on a first name basis. Bishop Romero was "Oscar" and Archbishop Chavez was "Luis." This idea of first-names-only carried forward for Joyce after the training and for the rest of her time in El Salvador. She always called Archbishop Chavez "Luis" and never made an appointment to see him. She would just show up at his office, and if he was there, he would see her. They would spend all day in the workshop and then an amazing thing happened. All 40 to 60 people attending the workshop would break into small groups of five to ten people and hit the road. They would all go out every night and visit a different parish and share the information from that day with the priests, sisters, and lay leaders of the parish. It is hard to imagine how many people they must have reached. This was evangelization!

Joyce came to deeply respect and love many holy people in El Salvador. One of them was the Jesuit priest Father Rutilio Grande. Father Grande was a young, smart Salvadoran priest. Joyce believed the sun rose and set with the Jesuits. She thought their leadership and example of giving their all in El Salvador was prophetic. An example occurred in 1989 when the six Jesuits were murdered and hundreds of Jesuits volunteered to take their places. Joyce said she would have to knock you out if you criticized the Jesuits. Grande was recruited to the priesthood by Archbishop Chavez and became friends with Romero in the seminary. He studied in Spain and for nine years taught pastoral theology in the seminary. He was one of many Jesuits who followed the ideas of the Medellin Document and gave up teaching in the seminary to live and work among the peasant people. Someone else could train the seminarians—he was called to be a pastor and to build Christian Base Communities. Grande had taken the same courses Joyce had at the bishops' Latin American Institute in Quito, Ecuador.

Joyce liked Father Grande for his very common way of simple living. He had the same great love of the people as Joyce did. She would often go to Father Grande for spiritual direction.

After Joyce left El Salvador, Father Grande became very involved in what he called "the pastoral option of liberation theology" and was an outspoken advocate for the peasants. He began to receive death threats, but his love for the people he served was so great that he stated with certainty, "I fear absolutely nothing in defending your interests, even if it were to cost me my life itself. To offer one's life for the love of one's neighbor is equal to what Jesus did. A person can do no greater act and people should hate no one that attacks him." Later he took the Salvadoran government to task for expelling the Columbian priest, Father Bernal. In his final homily he said, "Many people prefer a Christ of undertakers and morticians. They want a mute Christ, without a mouth, who passes them walking in the streets. Many prefer a Christ with a muzzle on his mouth. Many prefer a Christ made for our own whims and according to our interests."[1]

The following Saturday, March 12, 1977, Father Rutilio Grande was accompanied by 72 year old Manuel Solorzano and 16 year old Nelson Rutilio Lemus when the three were slaughtered by machine gun fire as they passed through a sugar cane field on their way to evening Mass. Father Grande was the first priest to be murdered by the military leading up to the civil war. Archbishop Romero went to retrieve his body personally. In a move opposed by many within the church, Romero canceled all the Sunday Masses in the Archdiocese except for one at the San Salvador cathedral. Over 100,000 people came to the Mass. It was there that Archbishop Romero began his outspoken criticism of the repression of the poor by the Salvadoran government that would ultimately lead to his own murder.

Archbishop Chavez was another person Joyce had a deep respect for. He was a tall, elderly, stately man that was loved by the people. He was supportive of the efforts by the local churches to ease the suffering of the poor. His support was critical to their work because not all of the Salvadoran bishops believed in this new liberation theology. But Chavez did, and he was down to earth and an easy man to talk to. Joyce also considered him a prophetic leader because of how he encouraged the sisters to have such a large role in parish life. Sisters had traditionally been involved in nursing, teaching school or housekeeping for priests, but in El Salvador they were doing it all. They were essentially priests without the ordination or the ability to do sacraments.

If you worked in a parish with 40,000 parishioners and only one priest, the need for sister and lay person involvement in ministry and leadership is obvious. So while they could not hear confession and give absolution they were doing spiritual counseling with parishioners. They were not saying Mass, but they were leading Liturgy of the Word services. They were demonstrating with the people, organizing Christian Base Communities, and leading all the activities of a parish.

Joyce felt that her role in all of this was prophetic as well. Joyce realized that, in many ways, she was the local presence of the pastor. She began to think if she was doing all of this, then she could be even more grace-filled if she could receive the sacrament of ordination as a deacon. After reflecting on this idea over a long period of time, one day she jumped on a bus to go downtown to see Archbishop Chavez.

She climbed the stairs to his office and told whoever greeted her that she needed to see the Archbishop. The Archbishop met her at his door and with a big smile said, "Ah, Joyce, it is so nice to see you." There was no kneeling down or kissing rings for Joyce, which was a common practice in those days, but there was instead a reply with an even bigger smile, as if speaking to a big brother, saying something like, "Luis, it is wonderful to see you as well." Knowing Joyce, it was probably not that short and considerably more creative. In any case Luis graciously escorted Joyce into his office. She did not beat around the bush, but got right down to business. She told the Archbishop all she was doing in the Santa Lucia Parish. He replied that he was well aware of her work and asked how things were going. She thought things were going unbelievably well. Joyce then explained she felt she could even do better if he would ordain her a deacon. This was not merely a bold request; it was even more outrageous when you realize at this time there were no permanent male deacons in El Salvador or the United States. The Archbishop smiled and said, "Oh Sister Joyce, you are so far ahead of us. You will just have to be patient." He went to a corner closest and brought out what looked like a gift of cheese and crackers he had received and gave them to Joyce, saying, "Please take this and keep doing the great work you are doing." The Archbishop could not grant Joyce's request, but he had treated her with the utmost respect and love. Joyce did not come away ordained, but she left the Archbishop's office feeling she had just been blessed in her ministry.

When Joyce first got to El Salvador, Father Oscar Romero was working in San Miguel where he founded an Alcoholics Anonymous group and also became the editor of the diocesan newspaper. The Catholic Church in Latin America went through a dramatic transformation as a result of Vatican II, the Medellin Conference, and all of the work done with liberation theology and Christian Base Communities.

Up to this point the Latin American Catholic Church's bishops and priests basically taught that your lot in life was God's will. So, if you were poor with almost no chance to improve your life, it was just God's will. If your husband had one or two mistresses and beat you when he was drinking, well, that too was God's will. You can understand why the dramatic change in what the church taught with liberation theology was difficult for many people to accept.

Violence was erupting across Central America as a result of the peasants' attempt to stand up for their rights. In Guatemala the violence started earlier than in El Salvador. Guatemalan Cardinal Mario Casariego's view was typical of how many in the Catholic Church saw the peasants' resistance—he was a staunch supporter of Guatemala's authoritarian regime and often was accompanied by a radio patrol car and two police motorcycles. In response to the murders of priests, he would say he knew of no murdered clergy even though most records said there were at least ten priests murdered. He went on to say, "If you mix in politics, you get what you deserve".[2]

The church in El Salvador was also closely tied to the wealthy, the government, and the military. Bishop Romero had been a chaplain for the military and had many close relationships with the military and the elite members of society. Religious, like Joyce, were aware of these ties, and when Archbishop Chavez announced his retirement, they realized Bishop Romero was likely to be their next archbishop. They were deeply troubled by this idea. When Romero was announced as the next Archbishop, Monsignor Urioste commented, "I was in Chiltiupan in a grassroots leadership course. 'We may as well forget it! That man is going to put an end to all of this!' another priest said to me. I hurried to San Salvador and sent a telegram to Archbishop Chavez, a farewell and job well done note. Then I sent another to Bishop Rivera, a note of condolence. He was the one we were hoping would be the Archbishop. I didn't send anything to Romero. I didn't congratulate him, because it wouldn't have been sincere on my part. I was deeply displeased."[3]

On the other hand, Romero was also closely connected to the peasant people. The people would flock to his Masses and many times the churches would be overflowing. When Joyce was at El Castaño, she attended a mission in nearby San Miguel where Monsignor Romero was speaking. Joyce remembers standing for hours listening to him speak. It was terribly hot, and the sweat was just pouring down, but no one moved while he spoke. Monsignor Urioste tells the story of when he first met Romero, who left him with an unforgettable memory: "We physically bumped into each other. Of course, I said hello to him, and he answered with a single word 'ayúdeme' (Spanish for "help me") something he said to everyone. I was impressed with his humility."[4] Urioste, who later got to know the transformed Romero, said he was a man of deep prayer and a man of the Church.[5]

Joyce had an opportunity while working with Father Jose Marins to help lead a workshop that Romero attended. It may be that this experience helped in the transformation of Archbishop Romero. But it was clear that the murder of his good friend Father Grande dramatically changed how he responded to the violence of the military. He called on both the military and the revolutionaries to stop the violence, but because most of the atrocities were carried out by the government his criticism of them was stronger.

Thousands of Salvadorans attended Romero's weekly Mass and listened to his homily which interpreted scripture in light of events in El Salvador.[6] He never ceased in his call for justice, and he became the voice of the voiceless. A few weeks before he was murdered, he said in his homily, "We want a church that is truly shoulder to shoulder with the poor."[7] Even though he had received numerous threats on his life, he continued his outspoken call for justice. In 1980 Archbishop Romero urged the United States to cease all military assistance to El Salvador. One month later the Archbishop ended his Sunday sermon with this plea: "I beseech you; I beg you, I order you in the name of God, stop the repression."[8] The following day on March 24th of 1980, at the age of 62, he was assassinated with a single rifle shot to the heart by the Salvadoran military as he was lifting the chalice while saying Mass. Six months later a full scale civil war began.

Joyce, for her part, stayed very busy during her last few years in El Salvador. While living with the Assumption sisters and ministering in Santa Lucia, she worked intermittently on two other projects. Both were with Monsignor Urioste. When Monsignor Urioste was asked to organize these projects, he said the only way he would do them was if he had Sister Joyce on his team.

The first project was conducting mobile rural leadership training. She called it "El Castaño on wheels." Joyce would sit in back, Monsignor up front with their driver, Raul, and they would head out early Monday morning to a rural parish and do all the same training she had done at El Castaño. If the parish was fairly close they would drive back to San Salvador that night and return to the parish the next day. If it was too far to drive back and forth, Raul would return to the city, and Joyce and Monsignor would spend the week at the parish. Most parishes and communities were poor, with no hotels or other accommodations. As you could imagine, sleeping on a church pew or whatever place they could find was not a comfortable proposition.

The mission work they and others were doing had transformational possibilities. A resident of the small canton, El Tronador, told the following story about a mission led by Father Grande: "Before the mission, the place was a mess. The canton was full of liquor and moonshine, sold illegally on every corner. People would get drunk and do stupid things. But after the mission, all that ended. No more drunken, disorderly behavior. The place changed in other ways too. Now we have collective projects, and even people who aren't involved in the organization offer to help out in some way. The people received the mission with open arms. After it ended, we were left with a whole bunch of trained Delegates of the Word, about thirty of them, all eager to work together. You could see the excitement in the people."[3]

Joyce told the following story about her trips with Monsignor Urioste:

Team Player

I was a team player on these trips, sometimes staying for a week in these outposts, sleeping on the church benches and arising with the roosters' call at 4 a.m. Warming our hands, I helped the mothers make tortillas alongside a barrel with logs burning.

Such love, enthusiasm, and such dedication is the way Jesus would do it today. Often we had no water, no showers; the outhouse was sufficient. We were into living the gospel; we were called communists and revolutionaries. I knew this was the Church's call. Monsignor Urioste read the signs of the times so clearly, and I followed, fearlessly trusting unconditionally.

The second project Joyce worked on with Monsignor Urioste was recruiting, training, and supporting groups of sisters for pastoral ministry in rural villages. Together over several years they recruited twenty-six teams of two sisters each to go live and work in the villages. Sisters who had only been teaching or nursing jumped at the chance to do more pastoral work in rural communities. Joyce would give them the initial training, work with them in the field as needed, and a few times a year she and Monsignor would do workshops for the sisters.

The sisters were doing almost everything the priests did except say Mass and give absolution; this included organizing and training of Christian Base Communities. This was really getting your hands dirty or "smelling like the sheep" as Pope Francis likes to say. Gustavo Gutierrez, who taught Joyce in Ecuador said, "It is women who for the most part have brought the base communities into being and kept them going. They have refused in the base communities to accept the second or third class citizenship the church imposes on them elsewhere. They may be denied holy orders, but they live holy lives."[9] Joyce's life has truly been a holy, Spirit-led life.

In 1976, after 13 years of mission work in El Salvador, Joyce decided to go on sabbatical. She was surprised to be leaving El Salvador because when she came, she was convinced she would never leave. But missionary work was changing and most sisters no longer spent their entire career in one country. Later Joyce would comment that her time in El Salvador was like genuflecting; one smooth motion of respect, love, and joy.

CHAPTER 6

Border Ministry

Today

Soon after Joyce returned to the United States, the violence in El Salvador escalated into civil war. Between 1980 and 1982 an average of 800 bodies were found every month. As a result of this violence and the lack of hope for a better life, it is estimated that up to 25% of the Salvadoran population migrated to other countries. Between 500,000 and 1 million Salvadorans migrated to the United States.[1] Many United States governmental policies, from supporting violent authoritarian governments in Central America to the North American Free Trade Agreement, contributed to the growing migration of people from Mexico and Central America. A good number of these migrants came to Iowa.

Harlan, the town we live in, has a relatively small Latino population. The reason for this is, of course, is jobs. The immigrants come looking for work, and Harlan only has a couple dairies and one food processing plant that attract immigrant workers. But Denison, a town just 20 miles away, has several large packing plants which do attract a migrant labor force. Back in 1980, both towns were made up of only white, mostly German third and fourth generation families. The population of Harlan was about 5,357 and Denison's was 6,675. By 2012 Harlan's population had dropped to 5,085 while Denison's had grown to 8,387, and that number may be low by as many as 2,000 because the immigrant population does not like to give their personal information to the census bureau.[2] How has one town grown so much while the other declined?

Back in the 1950's Denison made a decision to allow packing plants to locate in their community. In the early years the plants paid competitive wages with good benefits, but in the 1980's the workers went on strike and the companies decided to break the unions. It was an ugly time and ultimately the big packing plants won. Wages dropped dramatically from around $10.00 an hour for a regular line worker to $8.50 an hour. Benefits were reduced as well.[3] Breaking the unions lowered the packing plants' labor costs, but it created a problem as well. The local people were not willing to work in packing plant conditions for these lower wages, and the packing plants had to look elsewhere for labor. They aggressively started recruiting Latino workers. Once the word was out, immigrants came for the jobs. Today Denison's population is at least 40% Latino.

So which town chose the best path? Well, it probably depends on who you talk to. For the Latino immigrants, Denison is a good place to live. It's safe, has a good school system, and they can make a decent living. Denison's water tower proclaims, "It's a wonderful life," and compared to the communities where the Latinos migrated from, Denison, Iowa, is indeed a wonderful place. Of course they face prejudice just like all new immigrants. Some of the stories are disturbing, and it is difficult to understand how a person would bend over backwards to help their long-time neighbors in need but in the next moment treat their new darker skinned neighbors with so little respect.

If you're immigrating without the correct legal documents, just making the trip to Denison is a very dangerous undertaking. This risk really hit home to the people of Denison in 2002 when workers at a local grain elevator discovered eleven bodies in a locked rail car. The rail car left Matamoros, Mexico in June and was stored in Oklahoma for several months before being shipped to Iowa. The four women and seven men found inside the rail car suffered a horrible death.[4] In 2012, 477 immigrants died on the American side of the border as they tried to enter the country through very remote areas.[5]

One reason both Harlan and Denison's Anglo populations are declining is that there are very few good jobs for young people to return to after college. So just like the immigrants, our young people are leaving their home communities to find better lives. Our children are able to find these better opportunities within our own country, but that is not a possibility for Latino migrants.

In the Good Samaritan story[7] the lawyer asked Jesus, "Who is our neighbor?" Joyce had been serving our neighbors in El Salvador for the past 13 years, and now she was going to continue to serve them in Iowa, Arizona, and wherever else she was called.

---

[7]Gospel of Luke 10:29-37

Joyce was 40 years old and at a crossroads in her life. The Franciscan leadership asked her if she would like to return to school, but she felt no need for more formal education. She asked to be placed with a group of sisters "that don't run so fast." She ended up in a convent consisting of sisters from a variety of orders in West Point, Iowa.

Most people probably think of a sabbatical as anywhere from a few months to a year of prayer, study, and generally a break from whatever ministry a person had been doing. Sister's sabbatical did include a month's retreat with the Jesuits but the rest of the time was primarily spent helping a group of Catholic Workers open a new house in Fort Madison, Iowa.

Fort Madison is home to the Iowa State Penitentiary, a maximum security prison and part of a larger prison complex that today houses over 2000 prisoners.[6] With that many prisoners there was a real need for housing for the visiting family members. The Catholic Workers planned to provide a free place to stay for family members when they came to visit. The group was struggling to get their home up and running and Joyce was asked to go provide some leadership and organizational skill to help them put it all together.

The Catholic Worker Movement was founded by Dorothy Day and Peter Maurin in 1933 during the great depression. Today there are approximately 227 Catholic Worker Houses around the world. They are committed to nonviolence, voluntary poverty, prayer, and hospitality for the homeless, exiled, and forsaken.[7] Catholic Workers actively protest injustice, war, racism, and violence of all forms. Joyce spent a few cold winter months helping the Fort Madison Catholic Workers start their ministry serving the families of prisoners.

This Iowa winter seemed particularly cold to Joyce, but any winter would seem cold after so many years in El Salvador. A local priest, Father Honick who was involved in prison ministry provided her with his mom's old car to get her from West Point to Fort Madison. Occasionally, on particularly cold days, the car would not start. Fortunately the convent was right next to a Catholic school and the boys there loved to get out of school with the excuse of helping Joyce get her car started.

When the Catholic Worker house was up and running, it was time for Joyce to really get back to work. That work turned out to be as a hospital chaplain in Des Moines, Iowa. Since Joyce didn't really want to go back to school, the Franciscan leadership thought it might be a good idea for Joyce to have a second type of career on her resume. One of the best programs for Clinical Pastoral Education (CPE) was in Des Moines at the Methodist Hospital. The current CPE program is described as such: "Our programs provide an immersion in crisis, grief, meaning-making, and wholeness."[8] Joyce was willing to give it six months, but ended up staying with the program for two years. Joyce worked, as usual, very hard and held the same hours as the resident medical students. Not only did she work hard, but she and the other students were always analyzing their own lives. Joyce said, "It was horrible constantly digging around in your own head, exposing your innermost feelings." It was rather challenging for a self-described private person. But it was also very rewarding. She was assigned a floor and she worked with the patients just as their doctors would. She began the training with four other students and three supervisors. By the time she left she was one of the supervisors.

Joyce really enjoyed her work in the hospital. However, she became concerned that she was losing her Spanish language skills, and there was a growing population of migrants arriving from Mexico and Central America. She began to search for a job working with migrant workers. She found an advertisement looking for someone to work with migrant farm workers in Phoenix, Arizona. The Diocese of Phoenix had a Hispanic office, but they really did not have anyone working with the migrant farm workers who harvested the citrus and vegetables grown in the area. Joyce flew out for an interview, liked what she heard, but had to clear it with her leadership before she accepted. However, she was fairly sure she would get that approval, so sure in fact that she left one of her suitcases with her new employer.

You would be hard-pressed to find anyone who had to find a new place to live more often than Joyce has. Fortunately she had very simple needs. Joyce's total focus was on the people she happened to be serving at any given time or place. She did not want to spend one bit of energy on anything to do with housing, or anything else that took time from her ministry work. She explains in this journal entry:

Harmony

More so than ever, I choose to put an emphasis on God's love and to be fed by His word and His bread instead of wasting so much time and energy in caring for myself. I have made the decision to walk daily, minute by minute in harmony with the universe. This does open an entire new arena for me, alive and in love with all that is. Thank you, God for all those blessings that come my way with this connection to love.

She was fortunate to find a place to live at the St. Thomas convent. Most of the Sisters living there were Benedictine, but a total of six or seven different orders had Sisters living in the convent. The number of religious sisters had dropped dramatically over the last decade, and the orders were learning to work together.

It seems many times the jobs Joyce took were little more than ideas when she started. It was a good thing she was an organizer with such great energy. This job working with migrant workers for the Diocese of Phoenix was no different. The Hispanic office had not ministered to the migrant workers so they didn't understand their needs or even know where they were located.

Joyce asked, "How do I find them?" And the reply was, "We don't know, you have to find them." She asked, "What do you want me to do for them?" and the reply was, "You're their pastor." Well, this Joyce understood; after all she had spent years doing essentially that in El Salvador.

She started in late summer so the migrants were working in the grape vineyards. Each group of workers followed their own set of harvests. For example, the grape workers would relocate when grapes were done rather than wait for the citrus harvest to begin. She decided to name the locations so she could find them and know when people would be there. Finding the workers was always a challenge because at any time the owners would move them from one field to another depending on which field was ready to harvest. Another problem was that most workers were undocumented, so if a strange car pulled into a field the workers would disappear. Joyce soon worked out a signal with her horn so the workers knew it was Joyce. By the time Joyce had worked a full year she had about twenty different location names. All the names were related to the harvest or what the area looked like. For example she had the grape community, lemon community, green field community, and so on. She drew it all up on a map so she could always find her way back from year to year.

One of the first things Joyce had to do was get permission from the owners of the fields. Many of them were Catholic, and Joyce had orders from the Bishop, which helped. Truthfully Joyce would not take no for an answer and told the owners only want she needed to so that they would agree, and most owners did not object to Joyce ministering to the spiritual needs of the workers.

Because the orchard owners drove to Mexico to recruit their workers, most of them were men. Only once did Joyce come across a young girl, working with her dad. She dressed like a boy so you wouldn't notice she was a girl unless you got close to her. The life of a migrant was simply hard work. They worked seven days a week, slept under the trees, and just moved on to the next location when the work was done. The first year Joyce was there, the area received way above normal rainfall. Many of the men also slept under highway bridges and underpasses, but because of flash floods it was not safe. Typically dinner was cooked over an outdoor fire, but with everything wet this was not possible. Joyce distributed lots of bread that year.

Local parishes would donate things for the men. Joyce soon learned what was useful and what was of no value to the men. For example, at that time men's polyester slacks were popular, so Joyce received dozens of used slacks. But when she took them out to the field, the men would not take them. Lemon trees had thorns on them, so the men only wanted to wear blue jeans. She couldn't get enough blue jeans donated, so she worked out a deal with the local St. Vincent De Paul store and she bought most of their blue jeans for less than a dollar apiece. She worked to educate the people of the parishes on what the men needed, but they still would donate things like used toasters and other electric appliances even though there was no electricity in the fields or under the bridges.

It seems ironic that consumers in the United States demand low prices for food, which pushes retailers, producers, and farm owners to pay their workers' wages so low that people cannot live in dignity. Then we turn around and donate our old stuff to them because we feel sorry for them. The consumption mentality of American society always distressed Joyce and she was so thankful that the Franciscan vows included voluntary poverty.

Even though most of the orchard owners were Catholic, there were still worker abuses. In the late 70's and early 80's the immigration laws and border enforcement were not as tough as they are today. Orchard owners would actually take a truck down just across the border and bring back a group of undocumented workers to harvest their fields. When the harvest was complete, they simply called the border patrol, who swept in and deported the workers. The owners then would not have to pay them; all for the sake of lower prices and higher profits. Joyce discovered this to be a common practice, and this kind of abuse is still common today. A study in 2009 by a nationally recognized group of research organizations found that 37.1 % of un-

documented workers experienced minimum wage violations in the week prior to the study. The rate for men was 29.5 % and for women 47.4 %[9]

Joyce's day would start early in prayer with the other sisters. Then she had breakfast and made a stop at her office in the diocese's pastoral center just to let them know she was still alive and working. She worked whenever she was needed. For example, the vegetable workers harvested during the summer months, so they would start at 1:00 a.m. and work until whenever it got too hot to continue. So, Joyce made sure she was there when the workers were. Vegetable-picking immigrants lived in the area with their families and Joyce still remembers women picking with a small child hanging on one hip. Her job was to be their pastor, and she did so within the rules of the church. Instead of Mass she did communion prayer services. Instead of confession she was just present to whatever their needs might be.

Just like in El Salvador, sometimes their needs resulted from tragedy. One night she got a call saying one of the men she ministered to had died. They needed to get his body back to the family in Mexico. But with no money and no connections to the local mortuaries, the people didn't know what to do. This was not some project you could take a week or two to finish up; it was hot out and they had no place to store the body. But they called the right person; Joyce went immediately to a funeral home in south Phoenix. (Joyce says the poor Hispanic part of town always seems to be on the south sides of cities.) She went hat in hand, humbly, reverently, and maybe with a few tears, telling her story. The director said he would prepare the body, provide an inexpensive casket, have a showing in his parlor, and put the man's body on an airplane back to his family in Mexico. He would pay for everything, but if she wanted a religious service that would cost something. Joyce did not have any money, but because she ran the best wake service she knew they would not need someone to come in and do a service. Today, if you ever need someone to lead a rosary and prayer service at a wake, Joyce is the person for the job. When she leads the rosary, instead of praying the Mysteries of the Rosary with a pre-written text she will relate the Mysteries to the person the wake is for. Sometimes they can be quite funny stories if she knows the person well enough, and it is a great way to celebrate his or her life.

Once again Joyce became a mentor. The women's communities had a program called Shared Horizons where younger sisters or those changing directions would spend time with a mentor to learn about the ministry. Joyce frequently had sisters joining her when she went into the orchards. She also often had family come down and visit her while she worked in Florida and Arizona. Once when her parents visited Joyce was driving them into an orchard looking for the workers. She would stop and her dad would get out and open the gates feeling a little uncomfortable because there were "No Trespassing" signs everywhere. It was a beautiful day, but they could not find the workers; the owners must have trucked them to a different field. She said to her parents, "I guess we won't be doing church today," and her dad, who never swore but was unable to stop himself, said, "Let's get the hell out of here." Being a farmer himself, he would never trespass on someone else's property, but he was by no means the first person to do something out of character in support of Joyce's work.

Joyce loved this work. Here was a former farm girl working outdoors with simple, hard-working people—what could possibly be better?

A little history refresher might be appropriate to remind us how we got to this point with migrant workers. Texas won their independence from Mexico in 1836, and in 1845 joined the United States. The United States tried to negotiate with Mexico for the rights to what are now New Mexico and California, but started the Mexican-American war when those negotiations failed. After taking Mexico City, the United States government was able to negotiate the purchase of 525,000 miles of land with the signing of the Treaty of Guadalupe-Hidalgo in 1848.[10] Almost immediately there was a need for inexpensive labor as fruit orchards expanded between 1850 and 1880. Also the new railroad lines between Mexico and the United States created many jobs. It is estimated that at that time about 60% of the work force on these routes were Mexican.

World War I created more demand for migrant workers because of all the men were at war. When they came home from Europe, and during the Great Depression, migrants were pushed back out of the country. It seems as soon as there was little or no demand for migrant workers, something like WWII would happen and create demand again.

In 1924 the Border Patrol was created and the term "illegal alien" was born.[11] Joyce and the migrants were aware of the Border Patrol—occasionally someone would disappear, and Joyce would have to visit the local jails to try to find him. In the early days of her Hispanic ministries in this country, the enforcement was not nearly as tough as it is today. For one thing the Border Patrol did not have near the resources it has now, and beginning in the late 1980's a series of tough, deportation-oriented laws were passed. The budgets of the three enforcement agencies, Customs Border and Protection, Immigration and Customs Enforcement (ICE), and Enforcement and Removal Operations, have more than doubled since 2003 to more than $20 billion dollars a year with a staff of over 49,000 people.[12]

On one hand our society seems to be demanding low-cost labor to keep prices down and profits high. On the other hand, people don't want the immigrants in our country. It is hard to have it both ways. What would a just society look like?

Toward the end of her third year in Phoenix the diocese received a request from the Diocese of Orlando in Florida looking for help to start their own migrant worker program. Many of the parishes in Phoenix were now more involved in working with migrant workers, so they suggested Joyce help Orlando get their program going. Soon Joyce was living in Lake Wales, Florida.

The program in Florida was to be similar to the one in Phoenix, except they wanted it to be parish-based. It was to be a two-year contract for Joyce. The plan was for her to set up the program, train two sisters who would start the same time she did, and ultimately train local lay people to run the program.

In central Florida the migrant worker families spent the complete school year in Florida. They had enough work in the fall, winter, and spring to allow them to send their children to the local school system. In the summer they would first go to Georgia and then to Pennsylvania for the harvest of different crops. Joyce worked with the pastors from two different parishes where the ministry was based.

Joyce tells a funny story unrelated to her work that happened while she was in Florida. Her sister Virginia was visiting and the two went to a famous traveling passion play. The production recruited hundreds of local people to be the crowds in the play. It was a fantastic show held outdoors at night in one of the local orchards. After the play Joyce was driving home, got lost in the orchard, and then got stuck in some irrigated land. Then Jesus himself came to their rescue! Or rather, the actor who played Jesus found them and gave them a ride home. Virginia made sure everyone in the family heard that story and retold it at many a family gathering.

When Joyce first became a sister, her order's leadership gave, or at least helped their members, find assignments. But more and more that was not true. When her two-year assignment was up in Florida, she was once again job-hunting. Joyce was so open to the Spirit that it seemed new jobs miraculously came her way. This time the Spirit sent her to Memphis, Texas. A thread that runs through Joyce's ministry is the recurring roles of pastor-like positions. In Memphis it went so far that on her personnel records her title was Associate Pastor, and she even lived in the rectory.

The real pastor lived in Childress just down the road. He was responsible for two parishes, in Childress and Memphis, and one mission church in Turkey, Texas. He really wanted another priest, but since he could not get one, Joyce was the next best thing. These were small farm and oil towns in the panhandle of Texas. It was dry, windy, and hot, and Joyce says this is where she got to know the famous western tumbleweed.

As usual she did almost everything a pastor would do, and they rotated towns on weekends. When it was her turn, they had a Celebration of the Word service instead of Mass. She especially enjoyed the mission church in Turkey (Texas). It was a Spanish-speaking church, and it had a friendly, vibrant life similar to parishes in El Salvador. It was a great community where the people took care of everything. Every Sunday after the liturgy the parishioners would gather in the hall for a community meal. It was great fun for Joyce.

When they found another priest for Memphis, Joyce moved back to Arizona. She would work in or near Phoenix for the next eight years. Once again Joyce had an experience that demonstrates her openness to almost any housing arrangement. She was living in a two-bedroom house when a priest she was working with was approached by some Pakistani friends of his from Chicago about finding work and a place to live for their daughter in Phoenix. They flew down to Phoenix, and after meeting with them Joyce agreed to let their daughter, Betty, live with her. But before Betty moved, she and her family visited India. When Betty returned to the United States, she returned as a married woman. It seems the purpose of the trip was for her to be married to Shaji, the man her family had arranged to be her spouse. Shaji could not join Betty in Phoenix right away because of visa issues, but after a few months he joined Joyce's happy household. Joyce helped them find work, drove them to work for a time, and helped them buy their own car when they were able to afford it. Joyce was also blessed to still be living with them when their first baby came. It is not difficult to imagine the good times "Grandma" Joyce spent with Betty, Shaji and their first child.

Joyce worked for about a year at a home for battered women. It was a large operation with homes all over Phoenix. Abused women would come in sometimes all beat up with children in tow looking for a safe place to stay. It was a stressful job helping the women, while simultaneously trying to prevent those who did the battering from locating the women.

Next, she was off to be a pastoral assistant at the large "snowbird" parish of Holy Cross in Mesa, Arizona. In the winter months they would have a dozen Masses on the weekends to accommodate all the retirees who spent the winter in the area. Fortunately, they also had a group of retired priests who came down in the winter to help say all of those Masses.

Joyce's primary job was running the RCIA[8] program. But what she remembers most from her time at Holy Cross is the volunteer work she did helping immigrants fill out paperwork for the Reagan administration's amnesty program. She was surprised that immigrants who were applying for amnesty were not just from south of the border. She helped people from Canada and many other countries in their effort to become U.S. citizens. A little less than three million people took advantage of the amnesty law.[13] It is ironic that today the idea of amnesty is denounced by people on the far right despite it being their champion, Ronald Reagan, who pushed the 1986 Immigration Reform and Control Act through.

The end of Joyce's two-year contract at Holy Cross caught her by surprise. She happened to be attending an RCIA conference when the pastor called and

---

[8]Rite of Christian Initiation for Adults

said her time was up. Joyce mentioned to one of the other attendees that she was looking for work. This woman happened to work for the parish of St. Vincent De Paul, and she said they were, for the first time, looking for a bilingual person to run their RCIA program. Joyce exclaimed with a laugh, "Well you just go tell them you found the perfect person! She speaks great Spanish, has lots of RCIA experience, and is just a wonderful person." Well, that's exactly what she did, and within a few days Joyce had an interview, and by the end of that interview she had a job—another example of the Spirit at work.

Joyce loved the Vincentian priests who ran the parish. Phoenix was really growing at this time, and the St. Vincent De Paul parish was growing right along with it. A lot of the new parishioners were Latino, and the staff debated the best ways to reach out to the Latino community. Eventually they got a bilingual priest so they were able to add a Spanish Mass. It was here that Joyce became a local legend as the snow cone queen!

The parish had regular festivals and other fundraising and community-building events. A family had donated a snow cone machine to the parish and somehow Joyce was recruited to run the operation. It was hot, sticky work, but also loads of fun. You can imagine on a hot summer night how well snow cones would go over, and of course, you could not get anywhere near the booth without Joyce laughingly calling you over for a snow cone. Joyce spent five happy years here as the snow cone queen.

The same family who gave the parish the snow cone booth invited Joyce to go to Mexico with them for an extended stay when her work was done at St. Vincent De Paul. She spent three months with the family in a poor barrio on the outskirts of the vacation city San Lucas. While she was there, she did pastoral work in a senior care center and an orphanage. There was a very shy special needs girl in the orphanage who was always barefoot. Joyce always wanted to give her a hug but the little girl would always shy away. One day Joyce bought her a pair of bright red shoes. At first the shoes would stay on her feet for less than a minute at a time, but slowly and surely, not only did the shoes start to stay on her feet, but she began to warm up to Joyce. Sadly, Joyce's new little friend died a few months later, but Joyce still carries a warm space in her heart for the girl who always wore bright red shoes even as she rested in her small wooden casket.

Joyce took a bus from Mexico back to Phoenix. On that bus ride she had an experience that would, in a few years, lead her to border ministry. When the bus was about 30 or so miles inside of the United States it was stopped by the Border Patrol. The officers checked everyone's paperwork to make sure they each had a legal right to be in the country. A young woman with a small child evidently did not have what she needed because they pulled them off the bus and just left them on the side of the road. This was in 1993. At that time people could still walk across the border, go to work in the United States and at night go back home to Mexico. The border enforcement became much more strict twenty to forty miles inland, and Joyce supposed the woman and her child just had to find their own way back to the border town. Joyce felt terrible for the mother and her child and wanted to do something to help, but at the time there was nothing she could do. It inspired her to get involved with what she considered injustice at our border.

After that bus ride Joyce spent about seven years in prison ministry, which is detailed in Chapter 7. In 2000 she asked her leadership if she could leave her paid position as a prison chaplain and do volunteer border ministry full time. She had already been volunteering in her spare time with an interdenominational church group doing border ministry. In classic Joyce style, once she got the OK from her leadership, she decided she just needed to go down to the border and wander around to get herself educated. She would drive from Tucson down to the border town Nogales, park her car, and just walk around visiting with immigrants. Joyce journals about her experience in Nogales:

Towel Around My Waist

"It is quite a dream to think that one is a missionary. What is a picture of a day in the life of a foreigner on un-walked ground? Recently this border chaplain headed south and ended up at the Nogales border towns. What a shock to become aware of a daily reality here. How can people survive with outhouses and drinking water side by side with an over-supply of sewage all over the streets? Is this the servant missionary? Is this being able to see the light at the end of the tunnel? Is this seeing hope and living hope? Where are all of the sparks of hope now? Jesus washed the feet of the apostles and dried them with a towel. As I walk these new paths, I wear also the towel around my waist."

On one of her walks she stopped at a Baptist shelter that provided food and other basic services. The pastor recruited Joyce to teach English. So five days a week she would drive down to Nogales, teach English for an hour and then spend the rest of the day either walking around town or driving to other small towns in the area.

It turned out some of her old friends lived in a nearby town called Sierra Vista. They told her about a woman named Pat who for years had visions and conversations with the Blessed Mary. Pat's husband had built a shrine at a location and called it Our Lady of the Sierras. Two days a week they had healing prayers and there have been many reported healings.[14] The shrine includes a 75 foot tall cross which is a beacon to the immigrants who cross the desert there. Joyce would often stop to pray and visit with any immigrants that happened to be there.

The only rule the Baptist preacher gave Joyce was no proselytizing to the immigrants. It was his ministry, so that was only for him to do. Joyce had always given certificates as rewards for good effort. One day someone had given her a bunch of rosaries, so she gave those out as rewards to her students as well. But she had unknowingly crossed the line. That very day she was given her walking papers and told not to come back. Of course this was not the first time this sort of thing had happened, and Joyce always came away with a great attitude. She considered herself as having been sent forth rejoicing to tackle the next challenge the Lord had for her.

A Franciscan Sister friend of hers asked her to go with her down to Douglas, Arizona. Her friend decided not to stay, but Joyce did. She began to volunteer across the border in Agua Prieta at the Divine Providence Orphanage. Many orphanages in Latin America are not true orphanages in the sense that all the children lack mothers and fathers. Many times the parents are just very young, poor, and cannot provide for their children. In some places the children come to orphanages because they are the only places with a school they can afford to go to. At Divine Providence both were true. It was an all-girl orphanage with about 30 children, ages 3 to 14 living there. Almost all had someone on the outside who loved them, and weekends were quiet because most of the girls would go home. They also had a senior home with 20 to 30 poor older adults living in a different building, many of whom had Alzheimer's. Joyce thought it was perfect having the young children with the old folks, and she smiles at the memory of frequently seeing a young girl and a senior walking hand in hand. Here is a story from Joyce's journal:

In Private

When a four year old orphan comes up to you and says... "Could I speak to you in private, please Sister?" You look into those little eyes and take her little hand and move toward a bench under the tree. Now, what could such a little being have that is so heavy? How can a staff person in this orphanage not move quickly to give a moment to this little angel? Will the private time request be outside of my capacity?

As this adult mind holds these little fingers in my very large ones and feels weak, we walk together to the little spot in the yard. We sit under the tree on the little yellow bench and the little Sara sits very close to me and touches my arm. She rubs it back and forth in calm, satisfaction and hope. "OK, Sara?" I ask. "Sister, I just wanted to sit very close to you for a minute," she said. Tears came to my eyes as I wrap my arms around her and hold her ever so close.

Joyce's story about this little orphan girl reveals her great love and compassion for the suffering, lonely, and unloved. It is only natural for our hearts to go out to a child in need, but Joyce's heart went out to children, seniors, mothers, the incarcerated, and all suffering people who crossed her path. It is not enough to allow your heart to feel compassion for those in need. A person must first be with the people. Throughout the years of her ministry Joyce always placed herself in the presence of the same people Jesus constantly reached out to in His ministry. Joyce was first, physically present, and only then, could she serve the needs of the people.

One interesting side note was that Joyce came to respect motorcycle riders while at Divine Providence. There was a motorcycle club from Tucson that sponsored the orphanage. They would hold fundraisers, collect needed supplies, and come down regularly to deliver them. Two rich brothers led the effort. Joyce and all the residents would laugh with joy when the group came down at Christmas. Anywhere from 100 to 150 motorcycles driving in procession would arrive, bringing toys, clothing, and all kinds of gifts for young and old alike. They also brought the food for Christmas dinner and everyone had the best meal of the year. Joyce has loved motorcycles and their riders ever since.

Here is a journal entry that reveals Joyce's ever-ready compassion:

I Own This Place

"I have a favor to ask," says one of the senior residents to me as we stand in the yard at La Divina Providencia. "Could I have a bed here?"

"You got it." I said, "Come and I will show you."

"Thanks so very much. I knew you were kind," responded the senior.

With tears in my heart I walk, hand in hand, to the Asilo to show this 80 year old his bed. What a blessing I had just received from this elderly resident. My prayer is that I am 'so kind' always for this is God's work.

Having breakfast one morning in 2005 while Joyce was living and working at the Divine Providence orphanage, Joyce heard the news that Joseph Ratzinger had been elected Pope. She immediately was filled with distress and disappointment.

She believed women were already marginalized in the church she loved, and she envisioned it would only get much worse under Ratzinger's leadership. She was so distressed and concerned that she immediately went to the pastor of her parish at St. Luke's, and asked him for more of a role or job in the parish. After some thought, he put her in charge of the teenage confirmation program. She wanted to have a stronger connection with the church in the event that the new Pope would exclude women even more than they currently were. She felt a specific job in a parish would protect her place in the church. This is an amazing admission by Joyce, because she is such a positive person who will not say a bad thing about anyone even in challenging situations. We will leave it to our readers to decide whether her fears were justified.

Since her prison ministry days, Joyce had been involved with Episcopal Border Ministries. The group placed water barrels in the desert to try to keep the immigrants alive and hydrated as they crossed miles of hot and dangerous terrain. They would put a flag on a tall pole so the migrants could find the water stations. Joyce worked this ministry as a volunteer for over twelve years. Joyce wrote about a border experience:

Presence

My height immediately gave away that I was a U.S. person. With the Franciscan sister acknowledgment, the two border crossers welcomed the water and peace as we all sat there on the ground in the morning air. One could see just a short distance toward the west as the sun rose. Knowing that the water station was just 50 steps away, we stayed just to avoid being stopped by the border agent's cameras. They were located all over and showed migrant movement at all hours in the desert. These two migrants exchanged shoes with us, filled water jugs, received two extra t-shirts and they were off. "Someone is waiting for me in Oregon with a job," he said.

I just breathed, "Oh my God."

As the years passed, the border enforcement got tougher, forcing the immigrants to more and more remote areas. The number of people making the trip has declined, but the number of deaths in the desert has risen sharply. The result of our tough enforcement is a much higher mortality rate for those making the cruel trip to perceived prosperity in our country.

Every Tuesday at 5:15 pm in Douglas they hold a "Healing Our Border Vigil". Joyce and many others concerned about the violence and injustice on the border

would form a procession from the local McDonald's to the border. They would carry white three-foot crosses, each with the name of someone who had died in the desert. They would stop every so often to proclaim a person's name, pray for them, and place their cross against the curb on the side of the road. The crosses were so heavy they used grocery carts to push them down the road. The deaths in the desert and this Tuesday procession condemning the needlessness of the deaths continue to this day. Retiring members of this group are given one of these crosses as a parting gift and today Joyce proudly displays hers in her office.

Of course, not everyone agreed with Joyce's position on immigration. She would often, especially in the early morning hours, see men standing on their pickup trucks with night binoculars looking for any movement in the desert. If they saw anything they would call the Border Patrol to come and round up any immigrants they found. Fortunately Joyce never had any confrontations with these men, who were part of the Minuteman Project[9]. Joyce doubted if she could even give them the dignity of speaking with them. She expresses her frustration with the following journal entry:

Human Worth of Migrant

How can a just and humane immigration happen? All the time in all areas of our planet, people walk across the national borders to work, find shelter, safety, to reunite with family members.

My ministry is to be there with people on the move. Our mission is to encourage global solidarity. The charism is to work toward unity. Where

---

[9]Minuteman Project—a vigilante group working to prevent undocumented immigrants from entering the United States.

is the authentic security when I see so much fear and distrust?

So often there is a run from violence, poverty and war. Where are the U.S. lawmakers in all of these migratory challenges? I have seen the hope of migrants as one shares a 'care packet' in the desert of our Southwest. The basic human rights are hard to find.

Some would yell 'criminals' to undocumented persons in this country. Is our country a welcoming place for everyone? What happens to the "all are invited to the table"? Is the U.S. to receive the tired, the poor, and the huddled masses?

The group Joyce worked with built a sanctuary of sorts in the desert which offered food, water, clothes, and information. Joyce frequently had the opportunity to visit with immigrants as they passed through. She found them to be smart, determined, and prepared with a plan for where they were going. They would arrive at Joyce's sanctuary, battered from their journey across the desert. Many times they would be wearing flip-flops or some type of shoe that offered little protection for their feet. She often had to wash and apply a healing ointment and bandage their bloody feet. She came to disdain flip-flops. Joyce always sent them on their way with new boots or some kind of shoes that would protect their feet. Occasionally they were in bad shape and needed medical care at a local clinic. The volunteers ran considerable risk transporting immigrants to the clinic, and several were arrested and prosecuted for aiding undocumented immigrants. As soon as they were fed, rested, and their thirst was quenched, they continued their journey through the desert. Joyce often spent the night at the sanctuary. One thing that stood out to her about the experience was just how dark the desert was at night. Most places in the world have some kind of light pollution, but out in this desert it was unbelievably dark. Because it was so hot during the day many of the migrants traveled at night. Joyce could never understand how they could find their way. Joyce wrote the following about a sanctuary experience:

A Border Crosser

This young man, Pablo, came slowly through the desert sagebrush-seemingly looking well built, carrying a plastic jug and panting loudly. I raised our white and blue flag to let the movement in the desert know that there was a safe place near. These were water tanks that our volunteers placed around on these federal lands; (of course with permission).

Pablo's three layered clothed body was thorn full of desert cactus, wet with dew and his face blood-coated. I called out a welcome shout and my name, and he flew into my arms. How long we embraced, only God knows. Water, kindness, prayer, good wishes, food and a care bag and then 'Adios.'

Our water stations were scattered around the border areas, sometimes with volunteers. But most of the time crowded only with migrants; these were relocated at another spot to keep them more hidden from the cameras and border agents.

The undocumented immigrants Joyce encountered at the border were mostly men. Rarely a single woman or a couple would pass through, and never young children or teenagers without an adult. The dramatic migration of unaccompanied children from Central America to the U.S. in 2014 sent a message about the difficult realities of life for children in Central America. Some estimates conclude that in the year 2014 up to 90,000 children from Guatemala, Honduras, and El Salvador will attempt the treacherous journey to cross the U.S. border. In 2013 a delegation from Migration and Refugee Services of the US Catholic Bishops traveled to Central America to examine and try to understand the flight of the children. They reported, the absence of economic opportunity, lack of quality education, the desire to reunite with family members, and perhaps the greatest motivator was the violence and lack of security in their home communities, caused them to undertake the dangerous migration. The delegation recommended numerous ideas to protect the children including several addressing the root causes of the desire to migrate.[15] Joyce worked for 13 years in El Salvador on these very same issues. If the governments of El Salvador and the United States had supported the Catholic Church's efforts to allow people to improve their lives, there is a strong possibility we would not be experiencing the overwhelming migration of children today. With great sadness Joyce recognizes the injustice continues along the U.S. border and in Central America.

Joyce spent another year working in a small orphanage in Naco, Mexico. It was a busy tourist spot with lots of Americans crossing the border into town for a day of shopping. Her brother, Charley, and her sister's husband, Jerry, came down with some supplies for the orphanage and picked up more along the way. Charley did not want his car to cross the border. Being the conservative German farmer he was, he did not want to take the chance because he knew his car insurance would be no good in Mexico. But, of course, Joyce was driving his car, and the orphanage was in Mexico, so the car did have to cross the border. At that time it was an easy crossing with just a casual search of the car. As they drove on, Joyce turned to Jerry who was sitting in front and said, "Do you suppose he even knows we crossed the border?" Well, Charley did know, but he always supported Joyce even if he had to turn a blind eye occasionally.

Every other year, Joyce traveled to Wisconsin in the summer for her order's assembly. Joyce was seventy years old during the 2005 assembly, when one of the leadership asked her if she would ever consider coming back and working with the growing Latino population in Iowa. She really listened to this request and considered it an invitation from the Spirit; after all, this was how she always knew it was time to move on.

After considerable prayer she set a date for moving back in May of 2006. Her brother, Charley and her sister, Audrey flew down to drive back with her. Joyce always lived a simple life, so everything she owned easily fit in the trunk of her car. Joyce insisted on driving the whole way and considered it part of her grieving process for leaving her border ministry behind. She had lived and worked in the south for over twenty-five years. Sadly, a few days after the trip back to Iowa, Audrey died of an aneurism. Joyce was feeling guilty about Audrey spending a good part of her last few days with her, rather than with her family, but Audrey's husband, Denny said he could not think of anyone that he would rather have Audrey spend that time with than Joyce. That seems to be a common sentiment people have towards Sister Joyce.

CHAPTER 7

Prison Ministry

Today

Throughout her working life Sister Joyce has served the people that society casts off, the ones who must stay poor for us to stay wealthy, and the ones despised and pushed out of our sight. Scripture tells us that is exactly what Jesus did: "He has sent me to proclaim release to the captives, and recovery of sight to the blind, to set free to those who are oppressed."[10] These words tell the story of Jesus and who he came to serve. These are the same people that Joyce has served for over fifty years. Certainly the incarcerated men and women Joyce ministered to as a prison chaplain fall into this category. Joyce has also served people who were abused by unjust and broken political systems: not only the Salvadoran government, but also the United States immigration, criminal justice, and prison systems, which are equally broken.

Most people in the United States do not realize how unjust our prison system really is. Facts like these are widely unknown—we have more people in prison than any country in the world, even so-called authoritarian countries like China and Russia. Thirty-two states plus the federal government still have the death penalty even though the Catholic Church condemns it. European governments refuse to sell us the drugs to execute people because they believe the practice is barbaric. Our laws are also racially-biased. For example, African Americans are almost four times more likely to get arrested for simple marijuana possession than white people, even though they use marijuana at comparable rates. Clearly our criminal justice system is unfair and broken.[1]

The wars on drugs and tough 'three strikes and you're out' laws have filled our prisons to overflowing and have created a booming prison industry for private, for-profit prisons. Today in some states, like Louisiana, for example, there are people serving life sentences for marijuana possession because they got busted three times, and the 'three strikes and you're out' laws require judges to give a life

---

[10]Gospel of Luke 4:18

sentence. The irony is, if they lived in Colorado or Washington State, they would no longer even get a ticket for marijuana possession.

States are only now starting to review and reform these laws. Unfortunately, their motivation is more to cut costs, not because the laws are unjust. The growth in use of private prison and detention centers that house inmates and undocumented immigrants puts tremendous pressure on legislators to keep laws tough and incarceration rates high. Big businesses have invested heavily in the for-profit prison industry, and they are protecting their investment by lobbying congress.

In 2005, Department of Homeland Security started a program that requires the federal criminal prosecution and imprisonment of all unlawful border crossers. The program, known as Operation Streamline, mainly targets undocumented immigrants with no criminal history and has resulted in skyrocketing caseloads in many federal district courts along the border. From 2007 to 2008, federal prosecution of immigration crimes nearly doubled, reaching more than 70,000 cases. Incarceration can sometimes last up to 10 months or more, and it channels more than $1 billion a year in federal funds to privately run detention centers.[2]

Another example of how money interests influence criminal justice laws is that in some states sheriffs control the local jails and prisons. They get paid by the prisoner, and this money is a big part of their budget, so it is necessary to keep those jails full. This reality is a big motivator for sheriffs to lobby against any changes in unjust drug or immigration laws.

When Joyce joined the prison system as a prison chaplain, she quickly learned the harsh realities of how things work. She witnessed first-hand the impact of the war on drugs and later the toughening of immigration laws. She saw what happened to young men who entered the prison as non-violent offenders and spent years in the prison environment.

During her time ministering to inmates she lived a more isolated life than she ever had before. She did occasionally get to visit her community of sisters in Tucson, but not nearly as often as she would have liked. To keep her sanity, she began to journal. Joyce wrote most of the journal entries in this book during this time. These excerpts give an amazing insight on what was going through Sister Joyce's mind as she lived her ministry. Listen to Joyce's thoughts about prison ministry,

Alien?

I heard this past year that the prison ministry is alien. Over the many years that I have been involved now in detention ministry, I do not in any way consider it alien. Maybe this is a phrase that comes from those who have no involvement.

What is different between a poor, inner-city parish and prison ministry? It is true that most of the prison population where I minister is poor. One finds that they come from the underside of the American experiment: poorly educated, substance abusers with dysfunctional or non-existent families, or limited prospects. This population is not traditionally religious or moral in their lifestyles, but they are spiritual. Many are nominal Christians, some are superstitious and in the end one might call them unchurched. As I remember my years in the school system, I would have that these individuals are suffering from an arrested development. In so many ways, the needs and concerns are no different from yours or mine.

Something that I have in mind all of the time is the need to have good role models and how important affirmation of essential goodness is. It gives a sense of empowerment. Oh, you hear the question, "Is Prison ministry worth it?" "Are you saving souls or changing any lives?" What an unfair question. Is this the same question that you ask in any parish around the planet? What a false standard of success! Since all ministry belongs to God, its success is 'His affair.' It is as St. Paul says, "I planted the seed, Apollos watered it, but God made it grow." (1Cor. 3:6) My calling to be faithful to this mission is exciting, frustrating, messy, boring, and win-some-lose-some.

1993-2000

In 1993, Joyce was coming back from a few months in San Lucas, Mexico, and was once again looking for a job. She took the bus to Tucson, and spent two nights in a motel while talking to the staff at the chancery. She wanted to minister in a Spanish parish but nothing seemed available. However, she was heard by the Spirit, because they sent her to the Catholic Charities office in downtown Tucson. Catholic Charities knew what to do with this lone ranger who dropped from the skies. They needed a religious director for the jails and prisons. The person in charge of prison ministries was delighted to have some help; someone that was bilingual, willing to volunteer at the jails and prisons as a religious minister, and who would work only for a car, gas, and office space.

Joyce had gotten her first experience with prison ministry when she was helping at the Catholic Worker house. Father Honick, who had allowed Joyce to use his mother's old car, was the Catholic Chaplain for the Iowa State Penitentiary in Fort Madison. He asked Joyce to accompany him on his visits to the penitentiary, which she was happy to do. Now the Spirit was calling her back full-time to prison ministry.

In those days there was very little training and almost no paperwork, and before she knew it, Joyce was visiting the local jails and state prisons. She soon learned the "ins and outs" of prison ministry. There were lots of rules, and even though they presented a bit of a challenge for Joyce, she was a hard worker and her boss loved her.

Soon her boss told her about a position for a state chaplain job with the Arizona Department of Corrections. When Joyce hesitated, her boss said, "You're awesome," and encouraged her to apply. God was so busy pushing her along. She felt confident and so strong with positive energy that one dreary day, when all normal folk would have been home in bed eating popcorn, Joyce filled out the application and her boss mailed it into the Department of Corrections.

In no time, she was called for an interview in Florence, Arizona, at the Eyman Complex. The Senior Chaplain sat with Joyce for hours. He drilled her with so many questions that she didn't know if she even wanted the job. And Joyce had a few questions of her own: "If I take this job, when would it start? What does it entail? What are the hours, days, and salary?" The job description called for an ordained minister, which of course she was not. But for his purposes, a religious sister was considered an ordained minister. She made it clear that she could not say Mass. The mandated prison policy was "A Catholic liturgy weekly." He was flexible and after the long interview, he offered her the job.

She assured the Senior Chaplain of the Eyman Complex that she needed a week to contact her headquarters in Spokane, Washington, to get the 'OK' to take the position. What would her leadership of FSPA connected with the Department of Corrections say? They knew she was searching, and so she got a green light. Now she just needed to get a car and move near Florence, because she couldn't drive four hours each day back and forth to Tucson. She received their blessing for all of the above. Joyce's friend, Sister Rosile, who loved to negotiate big purchases, found a car for her and she got a lead on a small cottage. A secular Franciscan nurse was retiring from the prison system and she had a cottage in Coolidge. Everything was falling in place the way it always seemed to.

There were five cottages located out in the cotton fields near a golf course, just ten minutes from the Florence Prison. The Presbyterian couple, who owned the cottages, had one cottage empty. Joyce asked him if he would hold it for her, and she would pay him in a week. He said, "I know how you Catholic nuns work, you have a deal." He even helped her furnish the apartment with a table, some chairs, some dishes, and a sofa. The location was such a blessing for Joyce. She never missed a sunrise or sunset. It was her own little hermitage right out in the country. This was to be her home for a few years.

Joyce had to work with a wide variety of people in her career, and occasionally she ran into someone who did not appreciate what she was trying to do. Sadly, that is what happened when she tried to find communion hosts to take with her into the prison. The following story is taken from Joyce's journal.

To Catch the Stirrings of the Spirit

"I am a very quiet, humble, reserved and joy-filled person from a farm family in rural Iowa. "Simple Joyce," is what my friends call me. On the job, at the State Prison in Florence, Arizona, I needed to take into the prison on different days the consecrated hosts for the Communion services. There was one parish in this small town and so I made my way there one afternoon after work after phoning the parish priest that I would be there around 4 p.m.

I was awfully tired that day and had spent all day in the dungeons, wearing the metal vests and protective glasses. My body was all wet with the day's sweat. The parish priest led me into a small office with large, straight back chairs, a super large office desk and a leather chair where the pastor sat. He motioned for me to sit on the opposite side of the desk. Not one to waste any time, I had already begun to recall who I was, where I had come from, and what my gifts were. I was registered in this parish, and I had put my talents at the service of this small Catholic community.

The Reverend became uneasy and interrupted my communications and said that he was going to have the first word here. After listening for over an hour, he let me know that he was a canon lawyer and he was not available to do any Masses at the prison (the monster) across the street. Nor was he willing to do any reconciliation rights, etc. at the correctional facility. Worse of all, I was not free to take any consecrated hosts from the church without paying for them since the parish was very poor and with little income.

I was aching all over my body and began to feel like St. Francis pleading for the rule from the pope and cardinals in Rome. With the outpouring of tears, I slowly got to my feet and proceeded toward the door. Requesting that the pastor only think about my request (he was very moved to see the crying nun), he did promise to think about my need to take Communion with me to prison each day after Mass from here at the parish church.

On the following day, I was kneeling in the front pew of Mary of the Assumption Catholic Church and all of a sudden there was a touch on my shoulder. It was the priest saying, 'Anything you want, Sister, just ask for it.' The demon was confronted. Was it Mother Antonia[11] all over again in history? Yes, my heart was weeping at the realization of EVIL in our church, society and planet."

---

[11]Mother Antonio was an American Catholic nun and an activist who chose to reside and care for inmates at the notorious maximum-security LaMesa prison in Tijuana, Mexico.

Joyce comes across as a woman of constant joy and happiness, with the ability to shrug off any disagreement that happens to come along, and as a person who only shares her pain with the Lord. This is probably true for the most part, but she is very human and when rejection hurts those to whom she ministers, the pain is very real.

Occasionally Joyce was forced to ask for permission but over the years she developed a philosophy of dealing with priests and bishops as Joyce explains, "I've learned, don't ask questions or permission of priests and bishops. We don't need it. Vatican II said the power is not only in the priests but in the laity."

When Joyce went to work at the Eyman Complex there were five units holding men. Today Eyman has over 5100 committed inmates and the State of Arizona has over 41,000 in all of their prison systems.[3] That is actually lower than the United States as a whole, which in 2009 was about 743 per 100,000 people.[4] The United States imprisons more people than any other country in the world. Russia is second, and they incarcerate more than 600 per every 100,000 people.[5] Joyce was assigned a specific unit with which to work, but as the only Catholic chaplain, she also ministered to the population of the entire prison.

Her liturgy schedule was very structured because the prison wanted to know where every prisoner was every minute. Her actual liturgy services could be out in the yard, in the library or in the visitor area. The inmates had to request permission in advance to attend the liturgy. Inmates could also write a letter to a chaplain requesting a personal meeting. In theory it was the only way Joyce could meet with a prisoner one on one. But in reality, when she was in the prison cell blocks, people would yell out asking her to come to their cell, and it was just easier to visit with them right on the spot rather than waiting for the letter.

In 1997 Father Keith Warner wrote an article about Joyce and her work for a Franciscan Mission magazine. His descriptions of the prison and Joyce tell a great story, so we are reprinting it in here in its entirety.

"She's the Church!"

The servo-motor growled as it inched open the gate of perforated sheet steel underneath the sign that read "Double Lockdown Escort Pod." A piteous screaming came from the adjoining pod, which was under the supervision of a correctional officer immediately above me in a control booth that glowed with computer screens. As Sister Joyce walked into the pod followed by an officer, I clutched my bulletproof vest and safety glasses and wondered what manner of woman would want to be a chaplain in such a high-tech ultra-maximum-security prison.

Sister Joyce Blum (pronounced "Bloom") is a Franciscan Sister of Perpetual Adoration and a chaplain who works at the Arizona State Prison-Eyman Complex in Florence, AZ. Visiting the inside of an SMU ("special management unit") could overwhelm most people, but Joyce goes to work there five days a week. The Eyman Complex houses about 4,500 inmates, many of whom are in the windowless cells there because they caused "incidents" at other facilities. Altogether there are about 15,000 prisoners in five facilities in the Florence area.

"I see the prisoners as my parishioners," she says. "This is where I do my ministry. To somebody they are special, and to God they are special for sure."

Joyce draws on her extensive experience as a Franciscan Sister to help her in her ministry in Florence. A native of Panama, Iowa, she worked in Central America for fifteen years, and in Arizona and Florida in parish and migrant farm worker ministry. As she has deepened her desire to follow Jesus in the spirit of Francis, she has learned how important it is to recognize the humanity in all those she serves, even prisoners on death row.

"I respect all life," she says. "Prisoners don't come from another planet. They are people who belong to someone's family." Nevertheless, she recognizes that she has to rely on the support of others to find the strength for her challenging ministry. "I know the FSPA sisters are right behind me, and that some of them have been in prison ministry. This is working with the lepers of our society today, and this is where the Franciscans need to be. I feel like I'm, writing the fifth Gospel."

Because the Eyman Complex was built specifically to house many of Arizona's most dangerous inmates, Joyce and the team of chaplains there are not able to gather them for religious services. Much of Joyce's work involves visiting prisoners one on one. The prisoners are confined to their individual cells for most of the day, allowed to exit only under supervision for a shower, phone call or recreation. All three meals are delivered to each prisoner's cell. Cells are grouped into ten, forming a pod, and six pods are supervised by a control room which controls all of the motor-driven doors to the cells and pods. There is no specified "Death Row" in SMU-2, so the dozens of prisoners awaiting execution are spread throughout the unit. Some of the pods are inhabited by the most dangerous prisoners, and if Sister Joyce wants to visit them, she must be accompanied by a corrections officer.

Even though she is employed by the state, it is not easy for the prisoners to find out how they can see her or any of the other chaplains. She is not allowed to ask them if they want a visit; she has to wait for them to write her a memo. Once she receives an "inmate letter," she suits up in her bulletproof vest and safety goggles and heads out to the pods. At the same time, when she enters a pod, inmates often call her over to their cells.

Once she passes through the security system, she finds the cell of the prisoner who requested a visit. Inmates are prohibited from any physical contact with visitors, so Joyce speaks to them through the panel of perforated steel plate. Each cell has a panel about six feet high and eighteen inches wide with holes about the diameter of a pencil spaced every inch. These security measures may seem extreme, but inmates have been known to craft weapons out of virtually anything: hardened bread and glue become knives, and television cable wire and smuggled bullets become crude "zip guns."

At that point, she begins what she calls a cell-side worship service. "I ask them to start the prayer and they usually say something like, "Well, God, you know I've not been all too faithful, and I don't even know how to pray... Chaplain, you better take over." she explains. "So I will say, "This brother is in need of some help right now. Sometimes things happen in our lives and we land here in the hole. He needs to be heard, to release some of the things that are real deep in his heart." Sister Joyce is convinced that most prisoners have had some sort of spiritual experience even if they don't identify it as such.

"What I would call 'faith,' to someone else is a peace inside of themselves that they get connected with," she says. "With others, it's a love that they have shared with someone, or a relationship with nature. I try to get them to remember and plug into that."

Joyce tries to communicate a sense of human warmth and compassion, placing her fingertips over the holes in the steel panel, even though she can't really touch them. In the cases of extremely dangerous prisoners, the steel panel is reinforced by a panel of plexiglass, adding to the barriers. If the prisoner is Catholic and requests communion, she then passes them a consecrated host.

When I saw Joyce suiting up to visit prisoners in the pods, I was curious why she had a small tract, a religious brochure, about a subject that could be of no possible interest to any of the prisoners. After observing her first cell-side prayer service, I asked her why she thought an inmate would be interested in a tract about the ethical challenges of technology, and she laughed. Joyce then showed me how she slips a Eucharistic host into the tract and then passes it into the cell through the narrow slot beside the door. She prefers doing that to interrupting the prayer service so an officer can unlock the pass-through where meals are delivered into the cell.

Joyce tells a story which explains a little bit of what good can happen in the pods. "The other week I was cell-side, and after a visit I was going back down the stairs, and I heard someone shout, 'Who is she?' And this other voice answers, 'She's the Church! Don't yell so loud!'

"'Ma'am, can I talk to you?' I couldn't tell where it came from, because there is an echo in the pods. 'Which number, please,' I said, because all the cells in the pod are numbered. And he said, 'Would you come and pray with me?' 'My goodness, any old day I will. When would be good?' I responded. 'Well, I don't know.' These are the kinds of things that happen inside. I had no idea who this person was. I said, 'Listen, when you have that feeling that you want me to come by and say a prayer, or just visit, write me one of those inmates letters. I love to get those.'

"I could do that,' the inmate said, 'So you're the Church.' "They call us chaplains, here.' I said." She smiles.

Joyce believes that she is called to minister beyond the inmate population. She does not refer to the employees as "guards," preferring the term "officers." I try to support the prison officers in their humanity. They have a hard job. They are going to have to see me, because I am going to stand right in front of them. The officers are very respectful of me. This place is too serious and stressful for us not to support each other.

Beginning work at Eyman Complex SMU-2 was difficult. "I felt like I was going down in a hole when I went into the maximum security area. It was so hot and dark, I was just so wet with sweat. You know, it can get hot in Arizona!" She recognized that she was going to have to rely on the experience of other state employees. "During our orientation a deputy warden from Florence Complex told us: 'Just remember when you came into the gate, leave your own jacket right there and change jackets. And when you go home, don't take your work home with you, otherwise you will never last.'

"One of the hardest things about this job is making sure that I take care of myself, that I avoid burnout," she says. "I have to go to work calm and refreshed." Joyce lives in a cozy little cottage ten minutes south of Florence, nestled in among some cotton fields. "I love my little place out there! Some of it is the atmosphere, the open air, and some of it is never missing a sunrise or sunset. I am always excited about getting to work in the morning, but I am so excited to get back home!"

Joyce takes care of herself by holding to her commitment to prayer, her sisters and friends, and having fun. Praying keeps her going, and she is faithful to her contemplative life. She gathers regularly with the sisters from her congregation who are ministering in Arizona. Because she is halfway between Tucson and Phoenix, they occasionally meet at her place, shoe-horning themselves into her little house. On a free day, she usually heads out to Phoenix or Tucson to visit friends and recreate.

When I ask her about the parallels between her life and that of Sister Helen Prejean, made famous by the movie "Dead Man Walking," Joyce smiles, "I can't do a lot of the things that she did, because I am an employee of the state of Arizona. I can't contact family members or things like that. Still, the movie was a good one because you get to see the humanity on all sides."

I ask her, then, what she would say to those who support the death penalty, she replies, "Come and visit me. Come and spend a day with me. See, touch, taste and smell. I love it when people come and visit. You honor me when you come. When I walk through these gates, I see this as holy ground."[6]

A couple of years after Joyce started working, the state moved its death row inmates to Eyman. It was quite an operation. They only had to move them five miles or so, but they closed all the roads and moved them one prisoner at a time. They moved over sixty inmates without a problem. Joyce felt fortunate that not a single inmate was executed while she worked at Eyman.

Joyce wrote the following poem during her time serving death row inmates.

Execution

Execution

> Cries come freely.
> Pain a reality.
> Last meal...
> family visit.

> Change of sentence?
> No one hears.
> A chair is readied;
> injections prepared.

> A walk of death.
> A glance of 'Forgive me.'
> Silence....

But things did not always go that smoothly. Joyce often witnessed fights on the yard. Usually it had some connection to a game they were playing. For example, one time somebody pitching a baseball threw it too close to the batter's head and the next thing Joyce knew a brawl had broken out in the yard. Joyce's journal entry describes what a brawl was like.

A Sip of Water...

"This was a sad day at Minor's Yard . The chow hall erupted in fights. Nearly 75 inmates were laid out on the green lawn in the bright sun with the heat of the high noon temperature beating down on both staff and inmates. The inmates were all cuffed and pepper spray was all over the inmates, the officers and the air was stiff with the spray. The odor of the spray was evident.

It was one of those days that some racial explosion was bound to happen. Things around the yard had been hot since the beginning of the week. With so many inmates on the ground, there was time for them to think about what happened. Some of the inmates were being hosed off, eyes washed out with the running water and just being cooled off. Many were very uncomfortable and others were just lying in the grass waiting for the next order.

Soon a cart with a water container and cups came along and I offered to help give drinks to the handcuffed inmates on the ground. It had been a long time since I had given a drink to someone in a similar circumstance.

I broke up the sips just to be next to a couple of the guilty parties and to say a short prayer that they had learned their lesson. How many were being punished because a few minors choose to create a payback time at the chow hall with a fight.

It was obvious that I was not smiling as I went from inmate to inmate holding the water cup since they were all hands behind their back, hand cuffed. One of the minors said, "Chaplain, you are not happy about this mess, are you?"

"No," I said. "So just stay quiet and cool until you are told to move."

I felt that, I was giving 'living water' to the minors as they sipped the water and in three large sips had the paper cup empty. I recognized many of the inmates who came out weekly for bible-study groups. As the investigative team came on the yard, it was clear that now I was needed to help feed sack lunches to another 500-600 inmates and so off I went to respond to the Shift Commander request for volunteers. I got a cart filled with lunch bags and headed down to one of the houses. Ellen was with me and as we placed two lunch bags outside of each cell, some of the inmates watched us and called out a 'thank you!' I have always said that a person does not lose all of their manners when they come to prison."

Joyce tells about another time that as she was leading a Liturgy of the Word celebration for about thirty or forty men in the library when a lightning strike knocked out the power and the lights went out. It was pitch black in the room and the inmates started screaming and hollering just like a bunch of second graders. The lights soon came back on. Then Joyce told the men, that if that happened again, there would be no, sound from them. Sure enough the lights went out again but the men did just as she asked and didn't make a bit of noise. They finished the prayer service in the dark. When asked if she had ever felt threatened, her response was "No", but she did learn to watch her back and literally had to make sure she was not standing in a spot where somebody could approach her from behind without her knowledge.

Joyce could not absolve inmates of their sins, but often the inmates confided their innermost feelings and struggles to her as she notes in the following journal entry:

Pray For Me...I'm Slipping

"Pastor, can I come to church tonight?" We have a procedure here at the prison of choosing one evening a week to come out to give 'Praise and Thanksgiving.' "Sounds good," I responded, "But do check with the officer also." The minor was looking well groomed in his prison uniform—hair combed back neatly and eyes sparkling. The reality was... "It is my birthday tomorrow and I will be moving to the adult yard." "Oh, are you ready?" I knew how difficult it was to find yourself in a new location and considered a full adult. I could also see that his face was filled with excitement and also fear.

I walked into the little nitch where church was being held this evening. The blue chairs were looking so welcome as the young prison congregation began to approach and fill our little chapel. "Pastor, I have slipped this week... you better pray over me."

"Me too, Chaplain."

"Hey," I say. "What's happening?"

"Oh, it's my mouth, Chaplain. I know I have only one mouth but it makes more trouble for me than my two ears."

As usual in our evening church prayer, we prayed for healing and strength for this coming week. The birthday kid grew a foot during the prayer time.

Joyce was disturbed by the corruption she realized was happening in the prison. At Christmas-time Joyce and the other chaplains would go through the gifts from inmates' family members to look for contraband. She was shocked by what they found. Even though the prison had very thorough search procedures after family visits, it was clear lots of drugs were getting into the prison. She could only think some of the prison staff had been compromised. She also was aware of the practice of long-time inmate leaders forcing new inmates with desirable appearances to become their "boyfriend." Most of the men slept in a dormitory situation so it was easy for abuse to occur. If the men got caught fighting, using or selling drugs, or having sexual misconduct, they could be reassigned to a cell in one of the special units. Joyce spent a good share of her time in these special units.

Another sad day at Eyman came when a young man, who had only a few days left before his release, was murdered. It seems he had refused to do something for someone once he got out of prison. While he was sweeping the floor, an inmate in the shower left the door unlocked and slipped out and beat him to death. Joyce was on duty when it happened, and the warden asked her to go down to record department, get the inmate's contact information, call the family, and give them the news without the details of how it happened. Joyce did not know what kind of reaction to expect from the family, but when she spoke to the inmate's father, he asked what had happened. She said he would need to call back in a couple days for the details. The father did not seem surprised or angry, but he guessed what happened, saying, "Somebody got to him, didn't they?" Joyce had no answer for him.

The prison leadership tried to take away anything that seemed to cause trouble. They removed the weight lifting equipment, rosaries, or anything that could be used to make a weapon. They even removed the law books from the library because the inmates would research ways to get their conviction overturned or get new trials. They were filing lots of petitions in the courts.

In spite of all the trouble and violence, the inmates were always respectful of Joyce. Here is another excerpt from Joyce's journal:

What Do They Call You?

"What do the inmates call you on the prison grounds?" Well, it all depends. People do not know that I am a Franciscan sister nor do they need to know that information. I am hired as a state chaplain. I minister to all religious orientations with respect and dignity.

Inmates may say "Madam," "Reverend," "Minister," the "God Person," and "The Jesus Lady." Do I have a preference? Would it make any difference in my ministry there on the prison yard? It lets me know that I am living and showing the example of Jesus in my presence on the yards. What more can a minister ask for as they live out their mission? What is my relationship with Jesus? My presence brings God into these activities of counseling, listening, offering hope, etc.

St. Francis of Assisi a long time ago called his friend, Brother Juniper, and they together went out walking through the streets and countryside, 'preaching to the people.' They walked and walked without saying a word all day long. In the evening, Brother Juniper said, "I thought we were going to preach to the people and we never said a word all day." Francis responded, "Oh, but we did preach. As we walked all the people saw us and that made them stop during their busy day and think of God."

Francis goes on to say, "Preach the Gospel at all times, and if necessary, use words."

What a challenge to walk the Runs, and as I walk by, some of the inmates can be heard to say: "Shush, the chaplain is here," "Sorry Pastor, for swearing," "God Bless you Madam," or "Can I help you, Chaplain?" Like St. Francis my passing can remind all of God and they can react to the Jesus Woman according to the state of their own souls.

There was something about Joyce that earned the respect of inmates. Joyce always thought the chaplains were critical to the smooth workings of the prisons though they never seemed to get the appreciation they deserved from the top prison leadership. Maybe their value finally was recognized, because Joyce received the Employee of the Quarter near the end of her time as a chaplain.

There were 40 full-time chaplains employed by the State of Arizona when Joyce worked for them, and they often had time to visit about the state of the prison industry. The prison industry was a growth industry, and many of the new prisons were run by for-profit companies. Joyce thought this was a terrible idea. These businesses needed full prisons to make a profit and they needed new prisons to grow. The war on drugs had for many years fueled this growth, but in Arizona the new growth was coming from the incarceration of immigrants.

Joyce was beginning to wonder if by being a chaplain for the prison she was somehow supporting a corrupt and unjust criminal system. It did not help that the Senior Chaplain had the same concerns and in conversations with Joyce talked about the desire to maybe leave the system. Eventually Joyce's concerns about the United States criminal justice and prison systems, and her desire to once again minister to the Latinos led her to approach her Franciscan leadership. Would they would allow her to give up her paid position and do volunteer border ministry work? They did not believe in putting up road blocks for the Spirit to move, so of course, they consented. Once again Joyce was on to a new adventure.

CHAPTER 8

Returning to Iowa

2006

May of 2006 found Joyce coming home to Iowa. The Latino population in Iowa had grown tremendously over the last decade. They were not spread out evenly around the state; rather some communities, usually those with packing plant jobs, would have larger populations. Joyce was hoping to find a paid position in a parish ministering to the Spanish speaking community. Most of these communities were relatively small, and there were very few Spanish-speaking local people. Now that she was back at home she put her brother, Charley, to work helping her find a job. Here is what she had to say about her and Charley's efforts looking for work:

Broken

"Starting back on this side of the border, I would ask my brother to go with me to meet bishops, pastors, and different groups. I did not know how to be interviewed. This U.S. culture was so different. I would drive Charley's pickup to the different possible ministry persons. Upon arrival, I would have Charley go to the church and pray the rosary. After a long meeting, I left one place feeling good about the possibility of a Hispanic job and so I said to Charley as we began to drive home. "Let's pray a rosary." Poor Charley just responded that he had said three already. Such a brother."

Joyce ended up working in the Diocese of Sioux City where she worked at parishes in Carroll, Storm Lake, Denison, and Spencer over the course of five years. Then she moved on to the Diocese of Des Moines, where she first worked in Council

Bluffs and in 2010 moved to St. Teresa's Parish in Des Moines. Today, Sister Joyce is a mentor, not only to the staff at St. Theresa's, but also for the Shelby County Central America group.[13] Recently she was appointed co-vicar for the religious by Bishop Richard Pates of the Diocese of Des Moines. Her role as co-vicar is to support members of religious orders, and she takes special joy in mentoring the international sisters. Joyce has spent 51 years ministering to God's people—7 years in prison ministry and over 44 years in some sort of Hispanic Ministry.

"Work" is an important word when it comes to describing Joyce. She is a hard worker, as you might expect coming from her German farm background. The people of Shelby County are proud of their work ethic, and Joyce certainly lives up to their high standards. Now in her late seventies, this is what Joyce's day looks like at St. Teresa's.

A Typical Day for Sister Joyce

4:00 a.m. Alarm clock goes off, followed by coffee, getting dressed, and having a piece of toast. "O, Lord, open my lips...living faith."
4:50 a.m. Drive 10 minutes to St. Theresa's
5:00 a.m. Open doors to the church, prepare the altar and books for Mass, and water the plants if needed

---

[13]The Shelby County Catholic churches have a sister parish in Nicaragua. Sister Joyce is involved with the group's efforts in building relationships between the people of Nicaragua and Shelby County.

6:30 a.m. Meditation time

7:00 a.m. - 2:00 p.m. Eucharist, then ministry at the office, including taking communion to homebound parishioners. Help foreign clergy with English, the Missal, and homilies

2:00 p.m. Journal and quiet time

5:00 p.m. Walk and relax

When people think of Joyce, many might think of this spirited woman who is always laughing. Fun, with a great sense of humor, and full of laughter—these things are a part of Joyce. She does indeed include a little humor in most things. For example, recently she was visiting an elderly woman who had just lost her best friend. Joyce offered communion to her. The elderly woman said, "I haven't been to church in a long time."

Joyce replied with a laugh, "When you're pushing 100, the church comes to you. You don't have to go to the church." A comment like that, with a little humor thrown in to put someone at ease, is classic Joyce.

Barbara Woods, a liturgist in Des Moines, Iowa, wrote this letter:

"I am not a morning person. There should be a sign around my neck that says, 'Do not talk to me until at least 9 a.m.' Not so with Sister Joyce. She is up at the crack of dawn. In fact, she probably beats the dawn. How can anyone be so bubbly in the morning?

"One morning I had to come up to church early, I mean 6:30ish. Glancing over to my left, I saw someone walking quickly around the parking lot reading a small book. You guessed it...Sister Joyce. Weather permitting, she walks around a bit before the 6:30 Mass on the weekdays. Who knows what time her clock chimes? Maybe a clock isn't needed.

"When you arrive in the morning around 8:30, she has already walked, attended Mass, visited with a majority of people there, probably went to breakfast with them, made four or five phone calls, and is ready to go out the door to visit more people. As she scampers out the door, Joyce bids you 'Good Morning' with much enthusiasm and a great big smile across her face. You'll probably receive a big hug as well. She embraces people with the same energy she embraces life.

"Since the day Sister Joyce arrived, she has been bouncing here and there with so much energy that it is almost scary. St. Theresa's Church has its own 'Tigger' in Sister Joyce. How can someone her age and with her list of activities be so energetic? Well, you soon find out that her day, at least at the parish, ends at 3 p.m. I imagine she picked up the siesta idea when she spent so many years in Central America."

In 2012 when Pope Benedict and the Congregation for the Doctrine of the Faith criticized and sought to "rein in" the sisters' Leadership Conference of Women Religious, many American Catholics in the pews didn't agree. Their opinion was the women religious were doing the real work of the Church, doing what Jesus tells us to do, to care for the poor, to love. Sister Joyce's life and work are a good example of what sisters around the world are doing in their communities. She has never concerned herself with the careerism that Pope Francis so strongly condemns. She spends little energy on housing or any personal needs so that her focus can be totally on those she ministers to. Joyce has a spirit of joy, and happiness about her that can really be understood only when you get to spend time with her. Where does this come from? Joyce tries to explain in this journal excerpt from September 2001:

Bubbling Spirit

"You show me the path of life.
In your presence there is fullness of joy."
~Psalm 16.11

I am in very many areas today volunteering with many, poor and needy communities. People ask me at times. "How do you keep your bubbling spirit?"

This makes me smile for I know deep down how this happens. I am a Franciscan Sister of Perpetual Adoration. Since 1954, I am connected with the La Crosse, Wisconsin Franciscans. This bubbling spirit is a way of life for me. I was born on an Iowa farm back in 1936 with 6 sisters and 4 brothers. My mom and dad planted faith seeds way back in this rural community of Panama. I reap this honor and privilege today.

During the summer 2001, our Franciscan Community celebrated 'Sparks of Hope' in La Crosse, Wisconsin. This again invited our carefree spirits to run forward as brooks of deep life. I move in the fullness of life.

Many people think the Vatican's effort to bring the American sisters in line is typical of how the church treats women. Joyce has always felt strongly about women's roles in the church and in the world. Without women, specifically, Mother Mary, the church would not exist. Joyce witnessed a power in the women of El Salvador, a power driven by the Spirit of God to march against the terrible violence there. Joyce herself feels the power of that Spirit working inside of her. When people see Joyce lead a workshop or speak in public, they see this strong, confident woman, but inside Joyce is vulnerable and knows it is only by the grace of the Spirit that she can do what she does.

Yes, Joyce may feel some disappointment towards the meager role the Vatican allows women in the Church, and remember, she once asked an archbishop to ordain her a deacon. Even though he gently refused to do so, she has no time to get hung up on that "priest stuff." She is using her Spirit-led "woman's power" to do the work Jesus has asked her to do. Here is a reflection from Joyce:

Dreaming

"A need to develop a theology of womanhood"
—a quote of Pope Francis as he journeyed from Rio de Janeiro to Rome in July 2013.

Is there room for a deep presence for women in the church? Oh yes, not only as a wife, mother and altar servers. When I answered the Franciscan vocation in 1954 with the FSPAs in La Crosse, I knew that I would never be privileged to shelter another human being within my own body. It was a gift freely given. My deep relationship with my God invites me to be open to ever so many leadership roles. Can St. Francis and St. Clare give us a journey road? Pope Francis' recent words—"The Madonna is more important than the apostles, and the church herself is feminine — the spouse of Christ and a mother." He also proclaimed "Being Christian ultimately means not doing things, but allowing oneself to be renewed by the Holy Spirit." So, not doing, but being into transformation always.

St. Bede the Venerable would say, "Every day the church gives birth to church."

Sister Joyce Stories

We have given you, a small glimpse into the life and spirit of Sister Joyce Blum. Her love for Jesus, her Church, and the simple people she serves is a story worth telling. We close with a string of Sister Joyce stories from people who have come to know and love her. The first is a journal entry from Joyce which perhaps tells her story the best.

WELL DONE

When both my parents died, Mom in December 1993 and Dad in February 1994, I found myself standing at the caskets and my eyes were looking at their hands. Both times, the rosary hanging loosely, I saw hands that showed signs of hard work but at the same time, full of love. They were beautiful hands with long tapered fingers and at the end were well-formed nails. Dad's nails especially were so obvious these last years when I would find myself staring at those hands and wondering how blessed were those hands.

Both Mom and Dad were anointed with such artistic and creative hands. These hands held the beauty that only grateful sons or daughters would deeply know. Whether it was farming, gardening, making meals or driving the mules, at prayer or working late into the night after the six daughters and four sons were long ago asleep upstairs, these hands told lots about their total personalities and the way Mom and Dad lived.

I, too, look at my hands. There are similarities, large fingers, brown spots and tanned hands that possess a character that teenagers' hands lack. My hands too are used for practical things, daily chores, as well as, expressing my emotions. Whether, I have folded hands in prayer, sharing the Eucharist with the prison population, flinging hands in anxiety or hugging people that I love, I am letting others around me know who I am.

In Proverbs 31.20, I read, "A woman extends her hands to the needy."

The work of my hands gives me a feeling of fulfillment and of self-worth. Yet, I do know that there is a loving God who paves the way and I am not saved by my own hands. It is the work of God that saves me. It is His grace and my faith in Him that put my hands into service for Him.

Now, some 58 years of the work of the Holy Spirit is showing forth. My prayer is that no task is too great or too small to do. I pray that when I stand before my God, He will take my hands into His and say, "Well done, my servant... well done."

FOOD FROM HEAVEN (OR SISTER JOYCE)

Part of our team went on to visit Nicaragua when we were done visiting Sister Joyce's old stomping grounds. When we parted from Sister Joyce, she gifted us with a jar of peanut butter. Now, this was no ordinary jar of peanut butter—it provided safe sustenance when none could be found, was bilingual, made friends easily, helped those in need, and with fresh bread and local honey, truly was a gourmet food.

For example, imagine riding a local chicken bus (a bus for people and occasional chickens.) Just as you finish putting peanut butter and honey on fresh bread, the bus's money-taker sits down next to you, holds out his hand with a look on his face of "What about me?" Who could say, no, to that? So I handed over the honey and peanut butter slathered bread and made a best friend for the duration of our three hour bus ride. Lester, who of course spoke no English, took money, loaded stuff on the bus roof, took crap from no one, and made sure I was entertained for the ride. Lester had a secret handshake that only close friends, were privy to. I can't share the details, as I was sworn to secrecy, but basically it consisted of a handshake, a fist bump and a forearm smash. We shared our secret handshake every time he passed, and whenever he had time, he sat down and shared his life story. He liked his job, smiled often, and flexed his biceps for all the girls. Check out the attached photo of Lester.

We ran into a lot of people asking for money on our trip, and the last day we found another use for Sister's peanut butter. We were sitting down to our usual peanut butter and honey bread lunch at an outdoor park filled with people. An old woman approached and asked for help. Her eyes lit up as we started to spread peanut butter and honey on a slice of bread. She even gave us advice on how much peanut butter to spread on the bread. She left with a large smile, saying "'Gracias." We left the mostly-empty jar on the table hoping someone would get one last use out of Sister's peanut butter.

So you can see, this was no ordinary jar of peanut butter, and it really spoke to both Spanish and English-speaking people, provided for both us and those in need, made us several new friends, and truly was gourmet dining. Thanks, Sister!

We hope you have your own jar of gourmet peanut butter.

~ *The Authors of* A Heart Exchange

THE CHALLENGE OF INTERVIEWING JOYCE

Our team went to El Salvador with Sister Joyce to see the places she had worked in for a good part of her career. We also hoped to come away with a set of recorded interviews and a blueprint for the book we were trying to write. We didn't have a clue what we were getting into. First, our plan for our El Salvador trip was really no plan at all. The interviews, while helpful, seemed to not really get to the heart of Joyce or the truth of her experience. Joyce probably, like many missionaries, did not really want to share the details of anything that made her look saintly, important, or special, nor anything that made it seem her life was ever at risk. I am convinced that the reality is, if Joyce had stayed in El Salvador, she would have been murdered sometime before the end of the civil war.

Another challenge was Sister's tendency to not only like to talk, but to wander on to other subjects without giving a person a chance to get a word in. She probably thinks I am quite rude for all the times I interrupted her. I would start saying "Stop, stop, stop!", but she would have two or three more sentences out before she realized I wanted to bring her back to the topic; yet not one time did she let any irritation show at my interruptions.

I would call her up to four times a week and sometimes we would talk (I mostly listened, which my wife would have a hard time believing) for two hours. I would constantly bring her back to the subject and try to probe for more details or stories. Imagine trying to remember a story about your life from 30 or 40 years ago. Sometimes we just didn't get the story.

Our goal was to tell the Truth. In some places we tell some ugly truths about the U.S. government, people, and even the Catholic Church. But as you can tell by the references, we made a real effort to get to the truth. Of course, those things were not the story we set out to tell, but they had such an impact on the people Joyce ministered to that they had to be told to understand Joyce's life work.

Joyce does not easily tell about some of the more difficult truths in her story. The details of the horror and pain of searching with a woman for her husband or son in El Salvador, and worse yet the details of finding the body, or sometimes pieces of the body, is not an easy thing to reflect on, much less talk about. The reality of prison life where stronger men use the weaker for sex was not a pleasant conversation either, but the people Joyce serves are the outcasts, the abused, and the unloved.

There were many more truths about joy, happiness, laughter, love, and allowing the Spirit to work in her life. These things really are what make Sister Joyce Blum who she is. And while there are many stories along these themes, it seemed these were the harder ideas to really put down on paper. Hopefully some of the truth of Sister Joyce Blum came through. All the time with Joyce, all the phone conversations; to really get to know this Spirit filled woman; such a blessing for me.

~ *Tim Sullivan, co-author*

SHELBY COUNTY CENTRAL AMERICA PILGRIMS

In 2013 we traveled for the first time with Sister Joyce to Honduras. There were five of us, three women and two men. We had two rooms at the parish center so the three of us women shared a room together. I had to marvel how Sister woke up every morning and said, "Good morning, Jesus! What do you have planned for us today?" I could see then that no matter where Sister was, she and God were sharing the adventure.

In the little room the three of us women shared, we discovered there was no mirror. We didn't give it much thought until in the morning, when we were getting ready to leave for the day. I know Sister must have mentioned this little concern to God in her morning prayers. When we stepped outside our door that morning, there was a motorcycle parked just three feet away from our room, and of course, it had a rear-view mirror. The problem was solved. We laughed as Sister spoke the words we were all thinking, "Thank you, Jesus."

Wherever we went, Sister Joyce gave her heart to the people. She accepted their hospitality gracefully and extended her own whenever she had the chance. This caused her a little grief at one time during our visit, but she dealt with it well. Here is her journal excerpt on the incident:

> On our pilgrimage to Conception Village in Western Honduras, I was overjoyed at the rural family gathering to celebrate Eucharist. Hospitality was personified. This Franciscan beamed as she stood next to the altar and explained a most welcome invitation to visit her in her USA home, just as the families had done for her. Afterwards a very angry Sunday worshipper from the U.S. reprimanded her and let her know that she was not to invite the people to visit the U.S. A bit broken, I said, "I am a Franciscan. Mi casa es tu casa." (My house is your house.)

Sister's spirit couldn't be dampened—how could she be anything but herself? That is her spirit, always welcoming, loving and open to everyone. I thank Sister Joyce for passing a little bit of her spirit onto me and I hope to keep learning from this "Holy Woman."

~ *Charlotte Willenborg, co-author*

SHE IS THE CLAY

I live near the town where Sister Joyce grew up. I have gotten to know her and several members of her family in my forty years at St. Mary of the Assumption Parish in Panama. I had the privilege to accompany her to El Salvador in January 2014 for our pilgrimage. One thing that surprised me was that she didn't feel that she ever "fit in." There was always a search and question of fitting in. With her enthusiasm and energy that thought never would have crossed my mind. We reflected on many joys and sorrows throughout our journey and on the stories of her life. We prayed, we laughed, we giggled about mirrors and motorcycles. The Holy Spirit is a lot busier now that Joyce has convinced me "to just let the Spirit lead you and you will know what you are supposed to do." I believe she is in communion with the Master. She is the clay and the work of His hands....

~ *Patricia Graeve Michels, co-author*

CLIMBING TREES IN EL SALVADOR

As we entered into the middle of the trip, we had arrived at San Pedro Nonualco to spend the day with Monsignor Carpio. After showing us the town and his parish, he had arranged a place for us to stay at the sister's convent. By the time we arrived, it was already dark so the sister that let us in showed us around the convent while the other sisters prepared dinner for us.

We woke up early the next morning and since breakfast wouldn't be ready until 7:30, we had enough time for a short walk on the patio to collect our thoughts. As we were walking, I couldn't take my eyes off the three coconut trees in the backyard and I was entirely convinced that I could climb to the top.

During breakfast I mentioned that I wanted to climb one of those coconut trees. I didn't want to be disrespectful and climb without first asking permission, so I asked Sister Joyce if she would ask the sisters for me. After breakfast, Sister Joyce got permission for me, and we walked out to the trees so I could do my attempt. I was surprised to find a little kid at the top of one of the trees with his machete, cutting down coconuts. The sight of this encouraged me even more.

As I readied myself to climb the tree, I saw the other kid wasn't wearing shoes. I thought, "Yeah, I should do that too. It will give me a better grip and better dexterity." So I took off my shoes, wrapped my hands around the tree, and planted my feet firmly on the trunk in front of me.

Hands- check, feet- check, confidence- check.

I began to raise one foot and one hand, pressing hard on the tree with my feet and pulling hard on the tree with my hands. I made my next move and I learned quickly that this was much harder than I thought. Finally, I surrendered myself to the tree and the kid's superior climbing abilities. I hadn't even made

it halfway. After I came down, I realized that sometimes it takes a kid to show you a little humility.

Because the rest of the team traveled onto Nicaragua, Sister Joyce and I traveled together back to Iowa. Even though I was the youngest member of the team, Sister Joyce always accepted me as an equal member. My impression of her is "she doesn't view anyone as incapable of a good conversation. She loves to teach what she has learned, and she loves to learn from those around her." It was a pleasure to get to know her.

~ Patrick Sullivan, photographer

A SPECIAL GIFT: SISTER "JOY"

I met Sister Joyce when she took the position of Pastoral Care Minister at St. Theresa's Church in Des Moines, Iowa. She was looking for a place to live and I was ready to share my home. She came to my house with her brother, Charley to meet me. Upon entering, she gave me a huge hug. We chatted and after she'd seen the house, we discussed arrangements. I asked her when she'd like to move in. She replied, "Tomorrow would work well for me." I was a little aghast as I'd expected several days to get ready. This event was very indicative of the way she approaches life, "getting the job done." She begins each day very early with her spiritual devotions. She prepares carefully for each task. She has the ability to involve others, using their talents in many ways. Her name is perfect: Sister Joyce, so full of joy in her love for our Lord. Even her surname, Blum mirrors her enthusiasm and zest for life. The Lord blessed all of us in her calling, as she has responded in positively touching so many lives in varied cultures with her love, joy, and compassion. A special gift: Sister "Joy".

~ Margaret Zimmer, parishioner at St. Theresa's Catholic Church in Des Moines, Iowa

BEARER OF GIFTS AND STORIES

Reading Sister Joyce's writings are another story. Not only does Sister physically move quickly, but her mind moves just as fast. One can only imagine what is going on in the brain that moves at high speed and in two languages at the same time. Words just spill out onto the page and they come from the heart.

Journaling is a way of communication for Sister Joyce. She loves to write. When newsletter articles are due, her articles are usually in poetry fashion with some prose overlapped by a touch of the Spanish way of speaking. The basic thoughts are clear and beautiful; they may just need to be organized. Once you read the verses several times, you are able to visualize her thoughts, and get a glimpse of the beauty she sees in everyone and in everything.

The Spanish-speaking countries made a huge impression on Sister Joyce. At St. Theresa's, we don't have a large Spanish population, so Joyce reaches out to others in the diocese of Des Moines who need her help and guidance. I am never caught off guard when I hear her speaking Spanish on the phone, and then running off to meet the needs of someone who is not yet able to speak English.

A practice she continues, is the giving of gifts. When she meets someone for the first time, or if a special occasion arises, or if someone is lonely, Sister Joyce offers gifts. Sometimes she is asking the students to make things. Sometimes Sister Joyce spends hours making things. She loves to spend time on arts and crafts, especially if the items are going to make someone else happy. Many ladies of the parish have been drawn into her activities of making food, blankets, cards, party favors, paper flowers, decorations, and much more. Even the smallest piece of artwork is an important ministry in the eyes of Sister Joyce. These gifts speak volumes to those receiving them. They are gifts of love and support.

Her teaching skills have been rekindled as she shares the faith with the Spanish-speaking people in the area. Her storytelling unites the Spanish-speaking people with their families and ancestors in Central America. The school and Wednesday Faith Formation teachers frequently invite her into the classrooms to educate the children on the customs of those she has served, and to encourage students to become involved in the ministry. When she tells her stories, her face lights up and she becomes animated. You can feel the love and excitement she has for her ministry and the people she serves. They are stories of her family from all over, including her physical family in Panama. No one is a stranger to Sister Joyce.

Once in a while she speaks of her life in Central America, but she speaks with a heavy heart. The suffering and pain she witnessed and endured brings spiritual pain to her heavy heart like the Blessed Virgin experienced when she watched her Son endure His agony. The injustices that she observed bring tears to her eyes, but the will to fight for those unjustly treated, emerges. The death that surrounded her during that time has taken a toll on her body, as she too feels the pain and sadness. She knows that those who have died are with God in heaven, and those who suffer need assistance. Therefore, Sister Joyce advocates for the poor, especially the immigrants and the helpless. She is an 'angel of mercy.'

When she visits the elderly and the sick, she is a bright light, a glimmer of hope, and a connection to the parish. She goes bearing gifts ready to lift the spirits of those in need. Her words of encouragement give them a little strength to carry them through the day. The laughter and excitement she shares, lets them know everything is OK for the moment. Her witness of Christ brings them peace.

~ *Barbara Woods, Liturgist in Des Moines, Iowa*

GOSPEL JOY, COMPASSION AND LOVE

It was about three years ago that I first met Sr. Joyce. I had the opportunity to sit in on the interviews for the person I would be job sharing with for the Pastoral Care ministry here at St. Theresa's Catholic Church.

I'm not sure there was much interviewing to be done. Sister Joyce was not hesitant about talking! She immediately filled up the room with her vibrant, energetic and joyful personality. She told us a little of her background, which left us all with our jaws hanging open! Wow! She had so much experience in so many different areas, that we were left almost dumfounded. Why would she want this little part-time job at St. Theresa's? That was the question that intrigued us the most. Well, she told us. Her community had been supporting her in her missionary work for most of her life as a sister and she thought that if she could get a little paycheck, she could give something back to her community. Plus, she still had a lot of energy and lots to give... that was an understatement! I remembered feeling invigorated by her enthusiasm and excited about her positive outlook.

I remember the conversation after she left, "She is way over qualified for this job." We wondered if she would really want it. The answer was 'Yes'.

Well, it was just a few days later that she showed up with her brother. She moved in with one of our widowed parishioners and started right into work. This ministry was supposedly two of us sharing one full-time position. I quickly learned that Sister Joyce does not know the meaning of the word, "part-time". She gave her all to this ministry, working hard to learn the city of Des Moines and the people in our parish... especially the elderly and sick members. She has a deep belief in the value of all people, but especially the sick, poor and marginalized.

It was with some intimidation that I began working with Sister Joyce. After all, she had years of experience and much more education that I had. My fears were unfounded, as she was very humble, gracious and complimentary working with me. She actually acted like she was learning from me, while I know I was learning from her. But that is how humble she is, never arrogant or pretentious.

But that is how I see her spirituality...very humble. She has a deep prayer life which keeps her centered in God's Love and seeking God's will always. She desires to spread the Gospel with joy and compassion and love. She speaks to bring people closer to Christ, so that they may know God's deep and abiding love for them.

I have never heard her say one bad word about anyone. She is always able to see what is good in people. If she does feel frustrated about someone, she just says, "We will pray for them," which reminds me of how she thinks in the terms of 'we' or 'us'. She is very team oriented and seeking to always be inclusive to everyone, wanting them to know their value.

In working at Church, she always makes me laugh when she calls mothers "that dear mama." She sees mothers in the view of their motherhood being at the core of who they are and how they approach life. Even if they are not mothers, she believes all women are "mothers" in their care and concern for others. She also has a strong sense of the dignity of women, wanting always to uphold women and their inherent worth.

Sister has this wonderful ability to appreciate everything material, yet not be attached to it. She sees beauty in so much of the world, but desires so few material things. If some material thing does come into her possession, it burns a hole in her pocket, until she finds a home for it and gives it away.

Sister Joyce has been a gift to the St. Theresa's Parish community and myself. I will always be grateful for the opportunity to work with her, learn from her and laugh with her.

~ *Anne Dols, Pastoral Care Minister at St. Theresa's Catholic Church, Des Moines, Iowa*

NEVER MET A STRANGER

I have had the good fortune of getting to know Sister Joyce these past three years. We have gradually shared more of our time together. Sister Joyce actually sought me out... to see if our school kitchen had employment for a friend of hers (I worked in the school kitchen at the time). Shortly after that, she delivered a church bulletin to my husband and I while we were in the hospital for the birth of our son. More recently, Sister has given me private lessons to learn the Spanish language.

Sister Joyce is someone who can spread joy and energy. I smile when I think of her. Sister Joyce has become like family to us—my son and I call her "Madre Alegria." Sister Joyce is the type of person who has "never met a stranger." We have benefitted from Sister Joyce's generosity with both her timed and her treasures. In fact, my son has learned the word 'treat' from Sister Joyce because she loves to give him goodies when she visits.

Sister Joyce has helped me with more than just my ability to speak Spanish—she has shown me how to share love and joy with others. Sister Joyce has spread the love of Jesus Christ to our family.

~Angela Wolfe, young parishioner at St. Theresa Catholic Church in Des Moines, Iowa

PASTORAL CARE MINISTER

I first met Sister Joyce about three years ago when she applied in our parish as a pastoral care minister. Sister's resume was impressive with her decades of work in Central America among the poor. However, the position here involved visiting parishioners in nursing care centers, hospitals and the home-bound. I was concerned this might be a bit 'tame' for her, considering her past ministry. Sister Joyce assured me it would be just fine and she was right.

Sister Joyce has been and continues to be a great asset to our parish. I look forward to working with her well into the future, though I'm not sure which one of us will retire first as I have only 20 years to go.

~ Father Mark Neal, St. Theresa's Catholic Church in Des Moines, Iowa

RURAL PEOPLE

I had the privilege of traveling to Honduras with Sister Joyce on only one occasion but feel as if I have known her for all of my life. Sister Joyce and I share the historical legacy of growing up in one of the German Catholic "colonies" of Shelby County, Iowa. I grew up in the community of Westphalia and Sister Joyce in the community of Panama, about six miles to the west. We both grew up on farms. I have been a farmer for nearly all of my life (41 years). Thirty- one of these years have been as a certified organic farmer. I have always been interested in the plight of small family farmers as I have witnessed firsthand the gradual decline of small and medium-sized family farms in our own area over my lifetime. I found that I could easily relate to the condition of the small family farmers in Central America because many are facing some of the same obstacles we have but with so much more severity.

Sister Joyce has such an amazing love and "heart" for the people of Central America. She has given the gift of herself to the people of the whole region. Her gift of love for the adults and children of this region has meant working for social justice, for the betterment of family life and their faith communities, for the education of their children and adults,, and for the dignity of their daily lives.

Sister's sense of humor and warmth came through at every turn during our stay in Honduras in 2013. She told me in the community of Gracias that I needed to buy a pair of boots. After all, I claimed to be a "cowboy." (We raise cattle on our organic farm as well as a variety of other crops and livestock). So it turned out that I was given a lesson in bartering as I tried on a pair of boots in the market. I am still wearing these boots and they are "mighty fine" boots. Everywhere that Sister went, she began a conversation with whomever she met, bringing a smile to their face and a sense of solidarity with one another. She takes people as they are, and brings out the best in them no matter whom they are or what they do. This is another gift that she has brought to the people of Central America.

I have a great admiration for the farmers of Central America. They work very hard, for very little, for the most part. I have been in Honduras on three different occasions and have a great respect for their love, and care for the land that they work. Their small farming communities remind me in many ways of how I grew up in the farming community of Westphalia in the 1950's. There was a greater sense of community and solidarity and neighborliness than there is now. The competition for land and wealth is greater now it seems. The farmers of Central America face many of the same challenges and concerns that small farmers in poor countries face all over the world. This is the push to adopt the technologies and corporate controlled industrial model of agriculture that is the norm in America. This model incorporates high priced inputs of seeds, chemicals and fertilizers, consolidates land and resources into fewer hands, and does not recognize the food sovereignty or the ability of the peoples of Central America to grow their own food. This model looks too much to yields for export, not to bettering farm incomes with local market development, more reliance on cheaper and more sustainable use of natural resources, more diversity of crops and livestock species, and traditional lower cost, more ecologically sound crop and livestock breeding methods for yield and species improvement. If there was a real and honest effort with much more financial and people resources trained in sustainable agriculture, then perhaps more progress could be made in improving the quality of life in the poorest countries in Central America. I doubt if it is going to come with more Wal-marts, Cocoa Cola or Pepsi, which is what you see a lot of in Honduras.

Sister Joyce's work with Christian Base Communities is a great model for how the small farmers in Central America could begin to build a sustainable life.

If only the governments and big corporate interests would give them a chance. The Catholic churches in Shelby County Iowa hope to journey with the people of San Pedro Apostol Parish in Villa Sandina, Nicaragua in their efforts toward building economic justice.

I recently wrote the following poem about saving soil and seeds. It reminds me of all the seeds Sister Joyce planted in the people of El Salvador.

~Ron Rosmann, organic farmer, Westphalia Iowa

We Plant the Seed

We plant the seed but the harvest is not ours,

A speck of soil in our eyes, in our lives, in our time spent on the soil.

A speck of time in the eye of created time, we plant the seed.

We weep for the soil, so to the soil our speck returns, our bodies return, all bodies return.

We do not save our soil, so to the river our speck of soil goes, to the ocean where it weeps for us.

Sustenance for a future harvest that is not our own, we plant the seed.

We plant seeds so we might live, so others might live,

Who no longer stand on the soil, standing instead on cement

The hardened earth that will be ground up one day returning back to soil, we plant the seed.

The speck of soil in my eye sees the small Honduran farmer riding his small pony up the mountain to tend his soil, his seeds.

Seeds that carry the memory of tens' of thousands of years,

How long will they be his seeds, his brother and sister farmers' seeds?

The public seeds? We plant the seeds. We must save our seeds.

Who can really own the soil or the seed? Do we own the sun? Do we own our own name?

The speck of soil in my eye sees a hollowed out scarecrow watching over a hollowed out field,

Grown from seed for a harvest that is not ours to save.

We plant the seeds. We must save our seeds.

To be in communion, we strive to be, with the soil, with the seed,

With the art, with the science, with all creation. We are all farmers in our way.

We plant the seeds. We save our seeds.

Bibliography

CHAPTER 1

(1)   Robertson, Kenneth R. The Tallgrass Prairie. Illinois Natural History
        Survey; Champaign, Illinois
(2)   City Population. Iowa Data Center. State of Iowa, Des Moines, Iowa.
(3)   Preserving our Past, Ensuring our Future. Centennial Book.
        Westphalia, Iowa, 1997
(4)   Century Review Book. Defiance, Iowa, 1982
(5)   Portsmouth Centennial Book. Portsmouth, Iowa, 1982
(6)   Panama Pages of Time, Centennial Book. Panama, Iowa, 1984
(7)   Progress is our Future, Centennial Book. Earling Iowa, 1981
(8)   City Population. Iowa Data Center. State of Iowa, Des Moines, Iowa.
(9)   McSherry Breslin, Meg. Rev. Leo Arkfeld, "The Flying Bishop"
        Chicago Tribune, Chicago, Il. August 25, 1999

CHAPTER 2

(1)   Anderson, Thomas P. Matanza. Lincoln, University of Nebraska Press.
        1992
(2)   Buezo, Rodolfo, Sangre de Hermanos. Havana, Cuba 1936
(3)   Machón Vilanova, Francisco, Ola roja. Mexico, D.F. 1948

CHAPTER 3

(1)   Consalvi, Carlos Henriquez. Broadcasting the Civil War in El Salvador.
        Austin: University of Texas Press, 1992
(2)   Conference of Latin American Bishops, Medellin Columbia,
        September 6, 1968
(3)   Binford, Leigh. Peasants. Catechists, Revolutionaries; Organic
        Intellectuals in the Salvadoran Revolution, 1980-1992. Pittsburgh:
        University of Pittsburgh Press, 2004
(4)   Carrigan, Ann. Salvador Witness. New York: Simon and Schuster. 1984
(5)   McClintock, Michael. The American Connection Volume One Stat
        Terror and Popular Resistance in El Salvador. London, Zed Books LTD.
(6)   Anderson, Thomas P. Matanza. Lincoln, University of Nebraska Press. 1992

(7)   Conference of Latin American Bishops, Wikipedia; http://
        en.wikipedia.org/wiki/Conference_of_Latin_American_Bishops

CHAPTER 4

(1)   Marins, Jose. The Church from the Roots. Quezon City: Claretian
        Publications. 1983
(2)   McClintock, Michael. The American Connection Volume One, Stat
        Terror and Resistance in El Salvador. London, Zed Books LTD
(3)   Mongabay History. El Salvador 1988; http://www.mongabay.com/
        reference/country_studies/el-salvador/all.html
(4)   Komoska Mara. "Report for the New York Meeting Summer Session. "
        The Religious Society of Friends New York 2009
(5)   Carrigan, Ann. Salvador Witness. New York: Simon and Schuster. 1984

CHAPTER 5

(1)   Kelly, Thomas M. When the Gospel Grows Feet. Collegeville, Mn.
        Liturgical Press. 2013
(2)   Poitevin, Rene. La Iglesia y la Democracia en Guatemala. Anuario de
        Estudios Centroamericanos, Universidad de Costa Rica. 1990
(3)   Vigil, Maria Lopez. Memoiries in Mosaic. San Salvador: UCA Editores.
        2000
(4)   Urioste, Monsignor Ricardo. "A Saint for the 21st Century." A talk in
        2007
(5)   Urioste, Monsignor Ricardo. Personal interview with the authors, 2014
(6)   Kowalchuk, Lisa. The Salvadoran Land Struggle in the 1990's
        Cohesion, Commitment, Corruption.
(7)   Urioste, Monsignor Ricardo. Personal interview with the authors, 2014
(8)   Enemies of the War, A PBS Documentary, New Day Films
(9)   Brown, Robert McAfee. Liberation Theology. Westminister: John Knox
        Press 1993

CHAPTER 6

(1)   Castellanos, Teresa. Context for Salvadoran Immigration.
        Immigrantinfo.org
(2)   American Fact Find, U.S. Census Bureau
(3)   Personal interview by authors with former packing plant employees ,
        2014

(4)   Colson, Nicole. Victims of Washington's War on Immigrants. October 2, 2002

(5)   Anderson, Stuart. "How Many More Deaths? The Moral Case for a Temporary Worker Program." National Foundation for American Policy. March 2013

(6)   Daily Statistics, Iowa Department of Corrections. April 29, 2014

(7)   The Catholic Worker Movement, catholicworker.org

(8)   Clinical Pastoral Education, www.unitypoint.org

(9)   Bernhardt, Annette, Milkman, Ruth, et al., "Broken Laws, Unprotected Workers: Violations of Employment and Labor Laws in America's Cities," Center for Urban Economic Development, Chicago, 2009

(10)   Office of the Historian. Milestones: 1830-1860 "The Annexation of Texas, The Mexican, American War, and the Treaty of Guadalupe-Hidalgo," U.S. Department of State

(11)   Mexican Immigrant Labor History. PBS.org

(12)   Ewing, Walter A. "The Growth of the US Deportation Machine," Immigration Policy Center. April 9, 2014

(13)   Staff Article. "A Reagan Legacy: Amnesty for Illegal Immigrants." National Public Radio. July 4, 2010

(14)   Beal, Tom. "Pilgrims Come to Southern Arizona to Hear Virgin Mary 'Speak'," Arizona Daily Star. December 21, 2008

(15)   "Mission to Central America: The Flight of Unaccompanied Children to the United States." Report of the Committee on Migration of the United States Conference of Catholic Bishops. November, 2013

CHAPTER 7

(1)   "The War on Marijuana in Black and White." The American Civil Liberties Union, June 2013. New York, New York

(2)   Lydgate, Joanna. "Assembly Line Justice: A review of Operation Streamline," The Chief Justice Earl Warren Institute on Race, Ethnicity, and Diversity, UC, Berkley Law School, January, 2010

(3)   Inmate Committed Population, Count Sheet. Arizona Department of Education. May 12th, 2014

(4)   Correctional Population in the US. US Bureau of Justice Statistics. 2009

(5)   Walmsley, Roy. World Prison Population. Kings College London, 2009

(6)   Warner, Father Keith. "She's the Church." Franciscan Mission Magazine, July, 1997